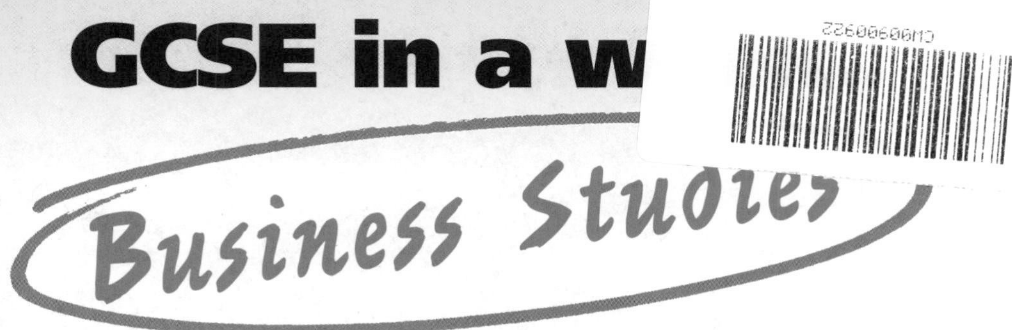

Nicky Small, Abbey Tutorial College
Series editor: Kevin Byrne

Where to find the information you need

Letts Educational
Aldine Place
London W12 8AW
Tel: 0181 740 2266
Fax: 0181 743 8451
e-mail: mail@lettsed.co.uk
website: http://www.lettsed.co.uk

First published 1998
Reprinted 1999

British Library Cataloguing in Publication Data
A CIP record for this book is available from the British Library.

ISBN 1 85758 9459

Editorial, design and production by Hart McLeod, Cambridge

Printed in Great Britain by Sterling Press Limited

Letts Educational is the trading name of BPP (Letts Educational) Ltd

Business environment

Test your knowledge

1 What are the four basic needs? ________________ , ________________ , ________________ , ________________ .

2 When basic needs have been met, consumers may spend money on ________________ .

3 What are the four factors of production? ________________ , ________________ , ________________ , ________________ .

4 When allocating resources it may be necessary to choose between two or more alternatives, for example, acquiring new premises or new machinery. What term is used to describe the alternative/s not selected? ________________ ________________ .

5 What occurs in primary production?

____

6 A mixed economy has a mixture of businesses operating in the ________________ ________________ and the ________________ ________________ .

7 If the price of a product decreases, then demand for that product is likely to ________________ .

Answers

1 food, clothing, shelter and water **2** wants **3** land, labour, capital and enterprise **4** opportunity cost **5** raw materials are extracted from nature **6** public sector, private sector **7** increase

If you got them all right, skip to page 5

Business environment

30 minutes

Improve your knowledge

1 Everyone has basic **needs**. These are: **food**; **water**; **clothing** and **shelter**. Few people provide for all of these needs personally, for example, by growing their own food, taking water from a well or stream, building their own home from materials collected or made etc. We rely on businesses to make products and provide services for us.

2 Most people have a limit to the amount of money they can spend, and this usually depends on the amount that they earn (**income**). Once basic needs have been satisfied, any money left over may be spent on **wants** or luxuries. People have many wants but will have to decide which of these to buy. A **consumer** is a person who purchases or uses a product or service. Businesses compete to encourage consumers to choose their products or services.

3 The resources needed to produce products and services are known as the **four factors of production**. These are: **land**; **labour**; **capital** and **enterprise**.

Land	Labour	Capital	Enterprise
▪ Physical surface ▪ Oceans, seas, rivers, lakes and their contents ▪ Items extracted from the ground, e.g. minerals, gas	▪ People employed in a variety of jobs	▪ Money ▪ Assets	▪ Businesses

4 Resources are limited. For example, there is a physical limit to the amount of land on earth, while a business may have a limit to the amount of money it has. Businesses have to make choices in deciding how to allocate their resources in the same way that individuals do. When a choice has to be made because of limited resources, whatever

has not been chosen is known as the **opportunity cost**. That opportunity has been given up.

5 There are three stages in production which are sometimes called sectors:

- primary
- secondary
- tertiary.

Primary production – **raw materials** are **extracted** from the ground or from nature, e.g. mining, farming, fishing.

Secondary production – construction takes place or where raw materials are **manufactured** or processed into a product. This often takes place in a factory, e.g. peas are processed and packaged. A product or a component that forms part of another product may be manufactured, for example light bulbs to be used in cars.

Tertiary production or commerce – finished products are sold or services provided, e.g. wholesaling, retailing (shops), banks, distribution. These services may be offered to individuals or to other businesses – services to trade. Direct services include teachers, doctors, nurses, dentists.

6 A **mixed economy** consists of state owned businesses – the **public sector**, and privately owned businesses – the **private sector**. The state or government also regulates the private sector through legislation.

7 **Demand** exists where a need or want is backed up by the ability to purchase the product or service. The demand for a product or service can depend upon many factors. One of these is price.

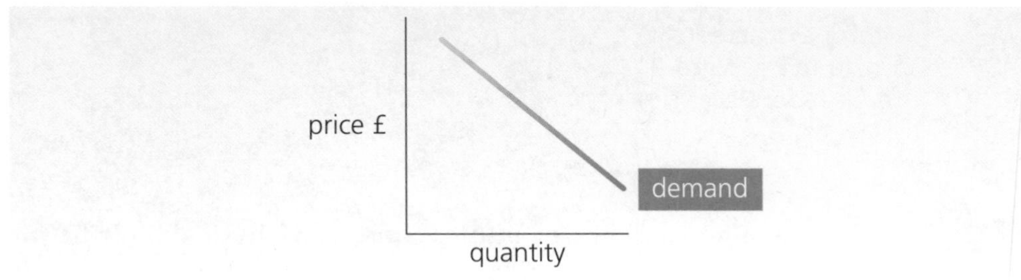

As the price **increases**, the quantity demanded decreases but as the price decreases, the quantity demanded increases.

The **supply** of a product or service also depends upon many factors. One of these is price.

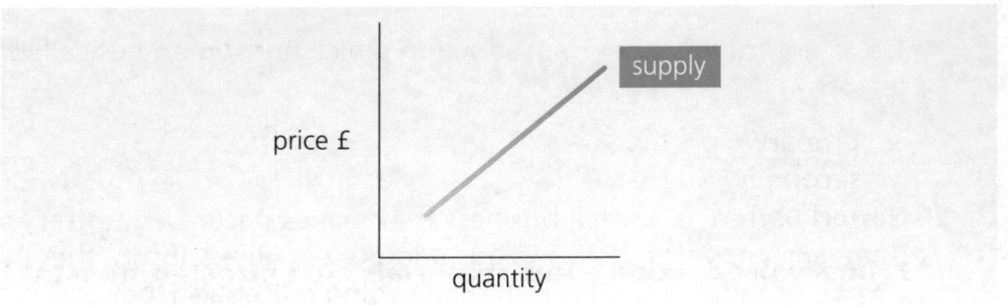

As the price increases, quantity supplied increases, but as the price decreases the quantity supplied decreases.

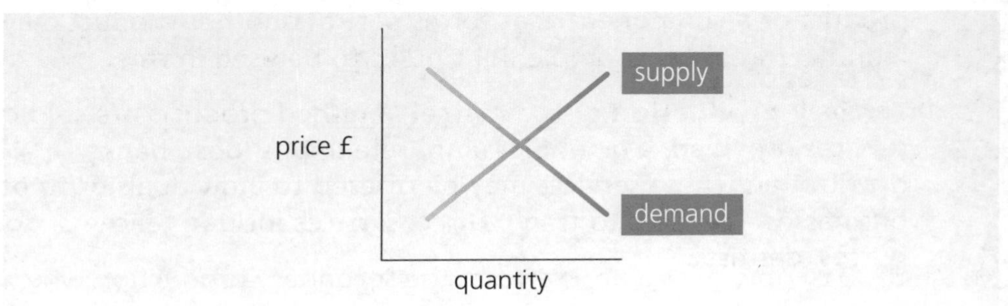

When the amount that the customer is prepared to pay is the same as the amount the supplier is prepared to sell at, equilibrium exists.

Now learn how to use your knowledge

Business environment

Use your knowledge

1 Gibson Pottery is a small business that makes decorated pottery items such as vases, bowls, mugs and plates. Alice Gibson, the owner, obtains clay, glazes and packaging materials from suppliers in the UK. Once made, the pottery items are wrapped in tissue paper and packaged in cardboard boxes. These products are distributed by a carrier to a variety of retail outlets in the UK.

a) Describe, giving an example, the primary production which takes place. *Hint 1*

____

____

b) Describe, giving an example, the secondary production which takes place.

____

____

c) Describe, giving an example, the tertiary production which takes place.

____

____

d) Pottery in Particular, a specialist pottery retailer, stocks Gibson Pottery. The owners have decided to increase the price of all Gibson Pottery products as they seem to be quite popular. What is likely to happen to demand for Gibson Pottery pieces? *Hint 2*

____

____

e) Alice Gibson wants to buy some equipment that would allow the business to increase the speed at which it produces the pottery. However, she also wants to invest some money in training her employees. After full consideration she decides to train her employees. What is the opportunity cost of this decision?

Hint 3

____

____

Hints and answers follow

Business environment

1 Primary also means first.

2 If a product you wanted to buy increased in price, would you still want to buy it?

3 Money is a resource, and resources are limited. What opportunity has been given up to spend money on training staff?

Answers

1 a) raw materials are extracted from nature, e.g. clay from the ground which will be used to make the pottery, wood from trees which will be used to make the packaging **b)** this is the manufacturing stage where the clay is used to make pottery / this is achieved through shaping, glazing and firing / the wood is made into tissue paper and cardboard **c)** the finished products, such as plates and bowls are sold in shops / the carrier provides a service, e.g. by transporting the products to the shops **d)** it is likely to decrease **e)** the equipment

Types of business

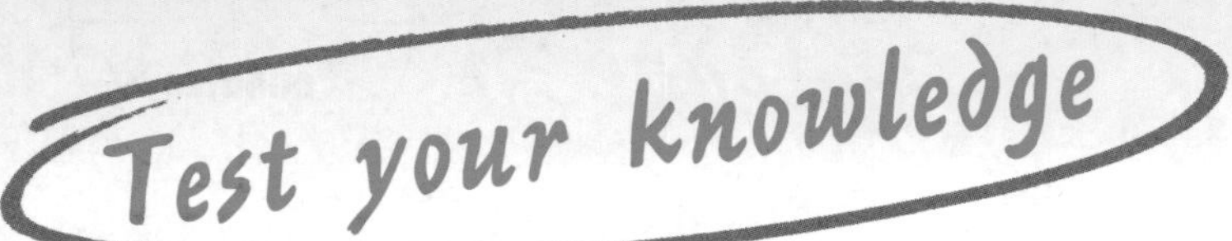

1. Who owns public sector businesses? ________________ .

2. Give two examples of public sector businesses.
________________ , ________________ .

3. State two features of a sole trader.

4. What are the minimum and maximum number of partners allowed in a partnership? ________________ .

5. What does unlimited liability mean?

6. What do the letters Ltd after the name of a business tell you?

7. What do the letters plc stand for? ________________ , ________________ , ________________ .

8. State three documents which have to be filed with the Registrar of Companies when forming a company. ________________ , ________________ , ________________ .

9. State two types of cooperative. ________________ and ________________ .

Answers

1 the State **2** National Health Service, BBC, Post Office **3** One person owns the business, owner usually works in the business, cheap and easy to set up, lack of continuity **4** 2, 20 **5** owners are liable for the debts of the business, personal possessions may be taken to recover debts **6** it is a private limited company **7** public limited company **8** Memorandum of Association, Articles of Association, Statutory Declaration **9** retail, worker

Types of business

Improve your knowledge

1 The **private sector** consists of sole traders, partnerships, limited companies (Ltd) and public limited companies (plc). Individuals own and control these businesses. The **public sector** consists of state owned services or businesses. Examples include the National Health Service, the Post Office, and local government. The BBC is a public corporation.

2 Since the early 1980s many businesses in the public sector, known as **nationalised** industries, have been **privatised**. This means that the business has been sold and become part of the private sector. Examples include, British Telecom, British Gas, British Steel. Privatisation helps to prevent monopolies and encourages competition.

3 **Sole trader**. One person owns the business, but the sole trader can employ as many people as he or she wishes. A sole trader normally works in their business. It is easy and cheap to set up this type of business as there are few formalities. If a sole trader does not have employees it may be difficult for the owner to take holidays or take time off if ill.

4 A **Partnership** can have between two and twenty partners. They are set up under the Partnership Act 1890 and are particularly suitable for doctors, dentists, accountants etc. It is important for partners to trust each other and have common objectives. A partnership deed can be used to set out the rights of the partners, for example if the profits are not split evenly.

5 Sole traders and partnerships have **unlimited liability**. This means that the owners are personally responsible for paying debts if the business goes bankrupt. If the value of the assets of the business is not sufficient to pay all debts, then the owner's personal possessions, such as his or her home or car, could be taken or sold.

Companies have **limited liability**. If a company goes into liquidation, the shareholders of the company are not responsible for paying the debts of the business. They will only lose their original investment and their personal possessions cannot be taken. This reduces the risk to investors.

6 **Private limited company** (Ltd). A company is a legal entity in its own right. It can sue and be sued. Shareholders own the business. A company must have a minimum of two shareholders, though there is not a maximum.

7 **Public limited company** (plc). There are similarities between a private and public limited company. The main difference is that public limited companies can sell their shares to members of the public through the Stock Exchange. One of the requirements to become a public limited company is that the company must have £50 000 share capital.

8 **Forming a company**. Founders of companies have to file the following documents with the **Registrar of Companies**:

- **Memorandum of Association** which contains the company's name, the company's address, the objectives of the company, a statement that the liability of the shareholders is limited, the amount of share capital. These details provide information relating to the company's external relationship with the outside world.
- **Articles of Association** states the internal rules such as how profits will be divided, how directors are elected, rights and duties of directors, when and how shareholders' meetings will be conducted.
- **Statutory Declaration** states that the requirements of the Companies Acts have been complied with.

If the registrar is satisfied, a **Certificate of Incorporation** will be issued. At this point a private limited company can start trading. A public limited company now has to raise capital. The company will publish a prospectus to attract potential investors. Shares are sold and once sufficient share capital has been raised a **Certificate of Trading** will be issued and the company can commence trading.

9 Other types of business include **cooperatives** and **franchises**:

Retail cooperatives – the Coop have members or shareholders. Anyone can join the Cooperative Society by purchasing shares, but these shares cannot be sold on the Stock Exchange. Each member has one vote regardless of the number of shares possessed.

Worker cooperatives are businesses owned and controlled by the people who work in them. All workers have one vote regardless of the amount of money invested. These are suited to small businesses.

A **franchise** operates under a recognised trade name, such as Body Shop. The franchisee agrees to pay the franchiser a sum of money in return for using an established name and image, and benefits from functions such as marketing and finance. It is less risky than starting a new business.

	Sole trader	Partnership	Private Limited Company	Public Limited Company
advantages	Retains control Accounts can be kept private Retains all profits Own boss Easy and cheap to set up	Share expenses, responsibility and decision making Accounts can be kept private Individual partners may offer specialism Continuity – partners can cover each other's absence	Limited liability May be easier to raise finance than sole traders and partnerships Management is shared Specialisation Continuity	Limited liability Easier to raise finance Can sell shares on stock exchange Specialisation Continuity
disadvantages	Unlimited liability Lack of continuity in event of death, sickness, holidays Not as easy to borrow money	Unlimited liability Disagreements between partners Number of partners is limited to 20	More expensive to set up than sole trader and partnership Shares cannot be sold publicly Accounts have to be lodged with Registrar of Companies – less privacy	Vulnerable to takeovers Shareholders receive some of the profit Annual accounts have to be published in full May have communication problems due to size

Now learn how to use your knowledge

Types of business

1 Louise Harris is a sole trader. She has owned her business for 12 years. Originally she opened one shop selling sandwiches, hot snacks, drinks and confectionery. The shop was successful and over a period of time, four more branches have opened. Although Louise is active in the management of all five branches, she is wondering whether the business should become a company.

a) State and explain **two** benefits of remaining a sole trader. *Hints 1/2*

Benefit ______________________________

Explanation ______________________________

____

____

Benefit ______________________________

Explanation ______________________________

____

____

b) State and explain **two** benefits of becoming a private limited company.

Benefit ______________________________

Explanation ______________________________

____

____

Benefit ____

Explanation ____

____

____

c) Louise tells you that she wants to expand the business further by opening more branches. Why could this influence her decision as to whether to remain a sole trader or to become a private limited company?

____

____

____

____

d) Louise feels that she needs more information in order to form a company. Describe the process which she would have to follow. *Hint 3*

____

____

____

____

____

____

____

____

____

____

Hints and answers follow

Types of business

1 Benefits in this case means the same as advantages.

2 The question asks what the benefits of **remaining** a sole trader are. Therefore a response such as it is easy or cheap to set up will not answer the question.

3 The following documents have to be filed: Memorandum of Association; Articles of Association and Statutory Declaration. Where do they have to be filed and what do they contain?

Answers

1 a) benefit retain control **explanation** a company would have shareholders who may want to make changes or disagree with Louise's ideas / as a sole trader Louise does not have to consult anyone else and can run the business as she wishes / **benefit** retains all the profit **explanation** a sole trader is able to keep the profit that the business makes, whereas if the business was a company the profits would belong to the company and shareholders would be entitled to their portion **b) benefit** limited liability **explanation** Louise would not be personally responsible for the debts of the business if it failed, her liability being restricted to the value of her initial investment / therefore her personal possessions could not be taken / **benefit** separate legal entity **explanation** the company can own assets, sue and be sued in its own right, which assists with continuity / other benefits include: management is shared; easier to raise finance; responsibility is shared **c)** it will be important to have money in order to expand / money can be raised through the sale of shares / the shares cannot be sold on the stock exchange or publicly offered for sale so it is likely that friends and family will buy the shares if they are interested in investing in the business and can afford to do so **d)** the following documents have to be filed with the Registrar of Companies: Memorandum of Association which details the company's external relationship with the outside world – it lists the company name, address, company objectives, the amount of share capital and that the shareholders have limited liability / the Articles of Association states the internal rules for the company and details how directors are elected and what their duties and rights are, how shareholders meetings will be conducted, how profits will be divided / finally a Statutory Declaration must be filed – this states that the requirements of the Companies Acts have been complied with / the Registrar will issue a Certificate of Incorporation if satisfied with the documents filed and the company can start trading

Marketing

Test your knowledge

1 When a business manufactures products that its consumers want it is said to be ________________ ________________ .

2 Finding out about consumer preferences is called ________________ ________________ .

3 Analysing the market to identify different types of customers is known as ________________ ________________ .

4 State four types of sampling. ________________ , ________________ , ________________ , ________________ .

5 What are the four components of the marketing mix? ____________ , ________________ , ________________ , ________________ .

6 A product's life can be lengthened by using an ____________ strategy.

7 What is the function of a wholesaler? ________________________________ ____ .

8 State three methods of pricing. ________________ , ________________ , ________________ .

9 Another name for above-the-line promotion is ______________ . Give three examples. ______________ , ______________ , ______________ .

Answers

1 market orientated **2** market research **3** market segmentation **4** random, cluster, quota, stratified **5** product, place, price, promotion **6** extension **7** a wholesaler buys from many manufacturers and breaks bulk offering goods to retailers in smaller quantities; credit is often available and orders may be delivered **8** cost plus, penetration, differential, psychological **9** advertising – television, local or national newspapers, leaflets, posters, radio, magazines

If you got them all right, skip to page 21

Marketing

Improve your knowledge

1 A **market** exists where buyers and sellers trade. Trading may be face-to-face, by telephone, in writing, by computer etc. Marketing is the process of getting the right product to the right place at the right time.

A business may be **market orientated**, where a business produces products or services their consumers need or want, or **product orientated**, where a business invents or designs a product then brings it to the market. If it is a good idea, other businesses may then imitate the product or modify it.

2 **Market research** enables businesses to find out about customer preferences and views. Few products or services are of interest to all people, so it is important to determine the **target market** – the people who will be purchasing or consuming the product or service. Market research may be carried out by the marketing department or by a firm of specialists who charge for their services. Information can be obtained through:

Primary data: data or information is gathered for the first time, e.g. finding out views on a new ice-cream. Primary data is obtained through field research, e.g. questionnaires, attitude surveys, interviews.

Secondary data: data or information which already exists. This information is found through desk research and may exist in retail audits, reports, company sales information, reference books or government statistics. Trade associations also carry out research.

3 The market is analysed to identify different types of consumers. This is called **market segmentation**. This can help to determine who the target market is. For example, in a market for books some consumers will want to read novels, some children's books, revision aids, textbooks etc.

Main methods of market segmentation are:

- **demographic** by gender, social class, level of income, age
- **geographic** by country, region, e.g. urban, rural
- **psychographic** by interests, e.g. cycling, lifestyles.

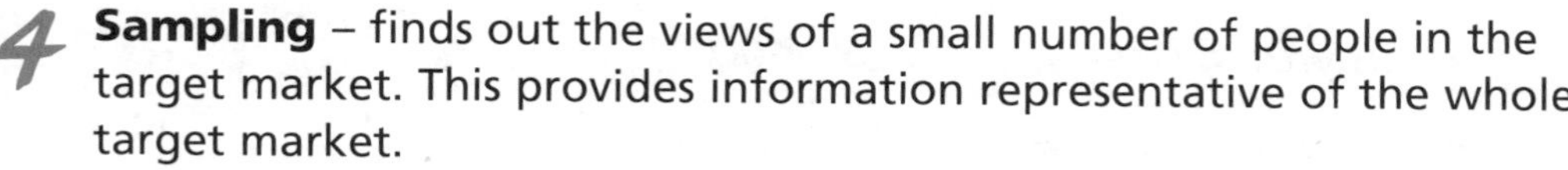

4 **Sampling** – finds out the views of a small number of people in the target market. This provides information representative of the whole target market.

Random sampling – interviewees are selected entirely at random, e.g. from a telephone directory.

Quota sampling – if a target market consists of 48% females and 52% males then a quota to interview will be selected in the same proportion. Once that quota has been achieved further interviews will not take place.

Stratified sampling – interviewees have a common link, e.g. female, between 18 and 25 years old.

Cluster sampling – a group or cluster of people are selected. This could be based on a town, street etc.

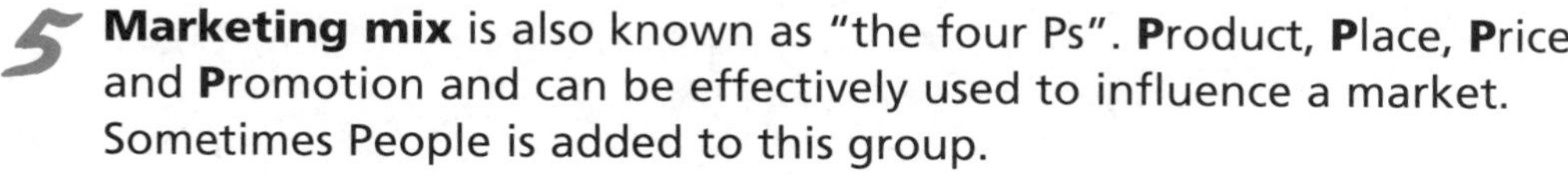

5 **Marketing mix** is also known as "the four Ps". **P**roduct, **P**lace, **P**rice and **P**romotion and can be effectively used to influence a market. Sometimes People is added to this group.

6 **Product**

This refers to existing and new products. In making decisions the following points need to be considered.

- Is it part of a range, such as shampoo for greasy, normal, dry hair?
- Does it have complementary products such as conditioners?
- What size is it / will it be? Will it be available in a range of sizes?
- Does it need special packaging to protect it? What information should be included on the packaging?
- How is it different to similar products? Does it have unique features?
- Does it require an after-sales service?
- What is the anticipated level of demand?

Product life cycle

The product life cycle demonstrates that all products follow a similar pattern:

- development from an idea
- introduction to the market
- growth in sales as a new product
- maturity as the sales slow down
- saturation where the market is satisfied
- decline when sales fall off.

This could be due to a change in fashion, launch of a superior product by a competitor or improved technology. Different products have life cycles of different lengths, some weeks or months, others many years. **Extension strategies** can be used to extend the life of a product. These could include product improvements. Make sure you can sketch a product life cycle.

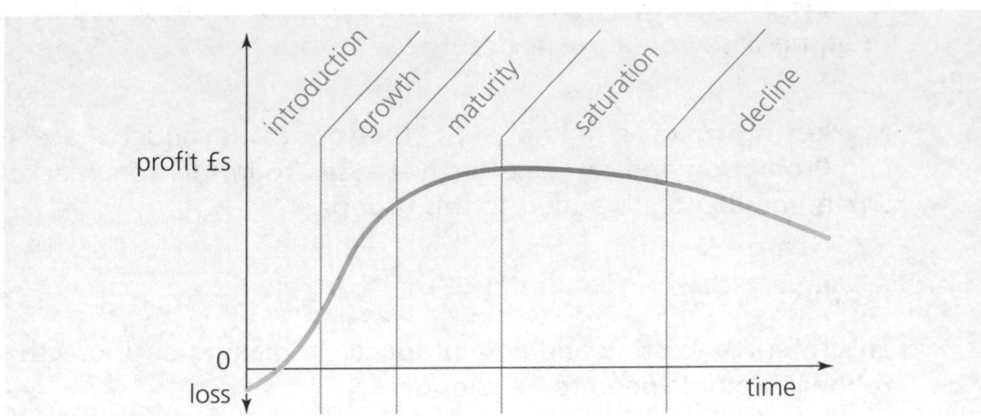

7 Place

This refers to the distribution of products and services.
Physical distribution: air, road, rail, ship.
Chain of distribution:

Functions of wholesalers and retailers

Wholesalers	Retailers
Break bulk	Break bulk, variety of products
Offer credit	Variety of payment methods
Deliver products	Expert advice and information
Offer variety	Prepare products for sale, e.g. fish

8 Price

The price the product or service will be sold at. Pricing methods include:

- **Cost plus pricing** – all the costs of making the product or providing the service are added together. A set percentage is then added, e.g. 30%. This ensures that costs are always covered.
- **Penetration pricing** – used when launching a new product. A low price is charged to encourage consumers to try the product.
- **Differential pricing** – where the same product is sold at a different price, e.g. rail fares are priced differently on different days, times and even months of the year; students, children and pensioners also benefit from lower fares.
- **Psychological pricing** – £4.99 instead of £5.00. This is an attempt to convince consumers that the product is cheaper. Many retailers no longer use this practice. Round numbers make calculations easier to perform and reduce the requirement for change to be kept in a till.
- **Loss leaders** – these are products that are sold at a loss to encourage consumers to purchase other items. This is an example of promotion and pricing being combined.

Promotion

Advertising above-the-line promotion – directly tells the consumer the desired message.

Advertising media include: television, radio – local and national, newspapers – local and national, magazines, leaflets, posters.

Media	Advantages	Disadvantages
Television	Reaches large audience Advert can be shown many times Adverts can be booked to fall before, during or after a programme with the same target market Moving images can be shown	Expensive Cannot look back at details If programme recorded on video the viewer may fast forward
National radio	Reaches large audience	Expensive Visual images cannot be used
Local radio	Effective if target market is local	Visual images cannot be used
Magazines	Specialist magazines can be used	May be expensive Images have to be static
Leaflets	Cheap, can be kept	May be discarded
Posters/billboards	Impact of size	Often unnoticed
National newspapers	Can be read again Reach a large audience	Adverts often black and white Adverts static Expensive
Local newspapers	Can be read again Effective if target market is local	Adverts often black and white Adverts static

Sales promotion / below-the-line promotion - consists of alternative methods of persuasion:

- **Sales** - products reduced, often used in fashion retail to clear lines.
- **Discounts** - 10% off, coupons, discount vouchers.
- **Free gifts** - free product with purchase, buy two get one free.
- **Samples** - opportunity to try a product.
- **Packaging** - packaging can be attractive or persuasive as well as informative.
- **Point-of-sale** - displays at the place where the customer purchases. This could even be on the counter, e.g. counterpacks, shelf liners, dump bins, posters.

Other methods include: sponsorship, competitions, after-sales service.

Now learn how to use your knowledge

Marketing

Use your knowledge

1 Ian Rodgers is a sole trader who sells take-away pizzas from a high street shop which is close to student accommodation. He has approximately 20 square metres of unused space that he is considering converting into a restaurant.

a) Before embarking on this venture he needs to conduct market research. Give **two** examples of market research suitable for his needs and explain why each is appropriate. *Hint 1*

Example 1 ______________________________

Explanation ______________________________

____

____

____

Example 2 ______________________________

Explanation ______________________________

____

____

____

b) Ian decides to proceed with this venture. State two methods of advertising the new restaurant and explain why each is suitable. *Hint 2*

Method 1 ______________________________

Explanation ______________________________

____

____

____

Method 2 ______________________________

Explanation ______________________________

____

____

____

c) Ian decides to use below-the-line promotion to encourage consumers to have a meal at the restaurant. He will offer **either** a free dessert with every main course ordered for the first week **or** 10% discount to students. Advise Ian which promotion to run, giving reasons for your choice. *Hint 3*

____

____

____

____

____

____

____

____

Hints and answers follow

Marketing

1 He would need to know if people would dine at the restaurant and if there is any competition.

2 Some forms of advertising are not cost effective for a small geographical area or target market.

3 The location is close to student accommodation. Who is the target market?

Answers

1 a) example 1 interviews with existing customers and passers-by which will ascertain willingness to eat in the restaurant / **explanation** if there is resistance he can find out why / interviews could be carried out with a questionnaire so that everyone is asked the same questions and the information can be easily analysed **example 2** survey of competitors / **explanation** he will need to know about other pizza restaurants in the area, what their opening hours are, how much they charge, the range of products offered and try to ascertain how busy they are / this will help him to decide on his product range, how much to charge / whether he can offer something different which will attract customers **b) method 1** advertisement in the local paper / **explanation** this reaches the local population who would be the target market / the advertisement could contain relevant information such as opening hours, address and telephone number, a sample menu and prices and details of opening promotions / it is cost effective **method 2** leaflets / **explanation** leaflets could be produced and delivered to houses and businesses in the town / these would reach the target market but may be discarded without being read / leaflets are easy to keep and pin on a notice board for future reference / they are relatively cheap and easy to produce / other methods include local radio, poster in window, poster at student accommodation, word of mouth **c)** either could be suitable / both offer an incentive to come into the restaurant and find out about the food and atmosphere / if happy, customers are likely to return

Production

1 Describe batch production.

____

____

2 A cost which remains the same regardless of the level of production is a ______________ cost. A cost which changes according to the level of production is a ______________ cost.

3 When total costs are the same as total revenue this is known as the ______________ – ______________ ______________ . If total costs are £5000 and fixed costs are £3000 what are the variable costs? ______________ .

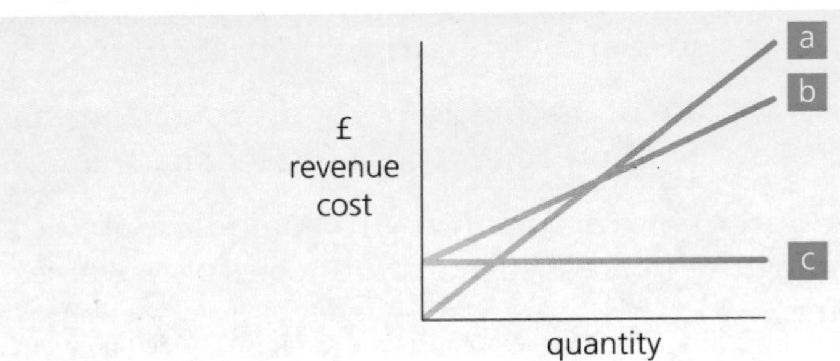

On the break-even chart above what labels should be given to

a) ______________ b) ______________ c) ______________ .

Answers

1 identical products are produced in small quantities or in a batch / each batch is completed before production on a different batch commences / this method is suitable for products which are made in different sizes and colours such as clothing **2** fixed, variable **3** break-even point, £2000, **a)** total revenue **b)** total costs **c)** total fixed costs

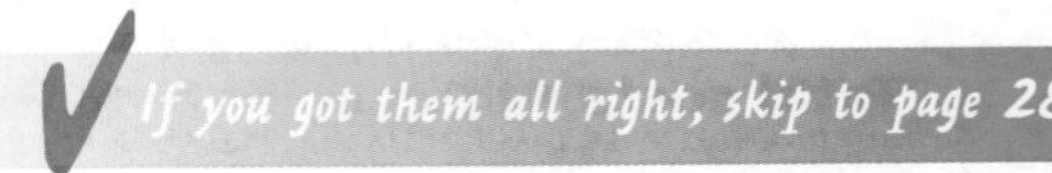
If you got them all right, skip to page 28

Production

Improve your knowledge

1 Methods of production

These include:

- **Job production** – products are made one at a time. Suitable for unique items such as paintings, made-to-measure suits, or very large products such as a ship or oil rig.
- **Batch production** – more than one identical product is made at a time but each group of products or "batch" is completed before another batch commences. This method is suitable for clothing and shoes where there are a variety of colours, sizes and styles.
- **Mass production** – many identical products are made on a production line. Machinery or employees each make or assemble a small part of the product before it moves to the next section of the production line. Flow production takes this one stage further where products move on conveyor belts from one process to the next.
- **Automation** – the use of machinery or robots to perform tasks. Automation is now widespread and has replaced many jobs.
- **Computer aided manufacture (CAM)** – computers are used to assist in manufacture in areas such as stock control as well as on the production line.

2 Costs in production

These include:

- **Fixed costs** – costs which remain the same regardless of the level of production. Examples include: rent, mortgage, interest payments.
- **Variable costs** – costs which change according to the level of production. Examples include: raw materials, heating and lighting, overtime payments, piece-rate payments.
- **Total costs** – the sum of total fixed and total variable costs.

Some costs contain fixed and variable elements, e.g. an employee may be paid a fixed salary but receive overtime or bonuses at times of high production.

Direct costs – those that can be directly linked to a production line or department, e.g. the salaries for the workers of a particular piece of machinery. Direct costs are often variable costs, but this is not always the case.

Indirect costs – cannot be linked in this way as, for example rent because every production line and department uses the factory. Indirect costs are often fixed costs but this is not always the case.

Total sales revenue – the amount of money that is received from sales of the products.

3 Break-even analysis

It is important for a business to know at what point the total costs are the same as the total revenue. This is called the **break-even point**. A chart can be drawn which shows how many units (output) have to be produced in order to break even.

When total costs are greater than total revenue a loss is made.

When total costs are lower than total revenue a profit is made. Profit and loss are explored in the chapter entitled *Profit and loss, balance sheets and analysis*.

To produce a break-even chart it is necessary to have details of the costs and revenues for different levels of output.

Quantity	Total revenue	Total variable costs	Total fixed costs	Total cost
0	£0	£0	£50 000	£50 000
50 000	£55 000	£20 000	£50 000	£70 000
100 000	£110 000	£40 000	£50 000	£90 000

A table such as the one shown above may have blank sections for you to calculate the missing figure.

Remember: total variable costs + total fixed costs = total costs

Therefore: total costs – total fixed costs = total variable costs.

Drawing a break-even chart

Quantity or units of output are always shown on the horizontal axis.

£s revenue / costs are always shown on the vertical axis.

Decide on a scale – look at the highest figures for revenue (£110 000) and total costs (£90 000) to find out the highest figure you will need to plot.

Draw in the fixed cost line – in this case the fixed costs are £50 000. This line will be parallel to the horizontal axis as it stays the same regardless of quantity. Don't forget to label it "fixed costs" or "FC".

Total costs have to start from the point of fixed costs (£50 000) on the vertical axis, so plot this point. When output is 100 000, total costs are £90 000, so plot this point. Draw a line between the two points plotted. Label this line "total costs" or "TC".

Use the same method to plot revenue, reading the figures from the table. Revenue always starts at zero. If nothing is produced a revenue cannot be achieved. Look at the highest figure for revenue – in this case it is £110 000 when quantity or output is 100 000.

The break-even point is where the total cost line and total revenue line cross. To find the break-even quantity follow this point down to the horizontal axis. Break-even revenue is shown on the vertical axis.

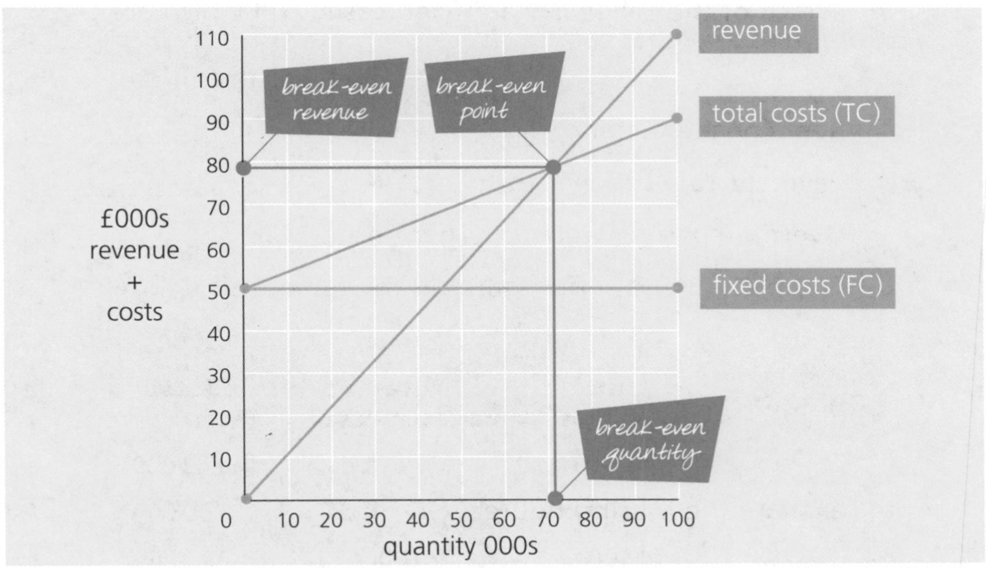

Now learn how to use your knowledge

Production

1 Mary Beary Ltd make toys. They have been continuously producing a doll called Eliza Jo for three years. Mary Beary Ltd plan to continue production for the forseeable future. Once the doll has been bought, accessories such as clothing and a car are available. The accessories available in shops change on a six monthly basis, but production of these items takes just one week per outfit. This ensures continued interest in the product and means that children in the same family can each have an Eliza Jo but have different clothes for it.

a) What method of production is suitable for making Eliza Jo? *Hint 1*

____

b) What method of production is suitable for making the clothes for Eliza Jo? *Hint 2*

____

c) Which of the following are fixed costs, and which are variable costs? *Hint 3*

	Type of cost
Rent for the factory	________________ .
Payment to a supplier for plastic	________________ .
Overtime paid to fulfil an urgent order	________________ .

d) Complete the missing figures in the table that follows: *Hint 4*

Quantity	Total revenue	Total variable costs	Total fixed costs	Total cost
0	£0	£0	£30 000	i)
50 000	£40 000	ii)	£30 000	£40 000
100 000	£80 000	£20 000	iii)	£50 000

Draw a break-even chart using the information in the table on the previous page.

Hints and answers follow

Production

1 The doll has been manufactured continuously and will be for the foreseeable future.

2 Each outfit can be made in a week and is not repeated.

3 Variable costs vary according to the level of production.

4 Fixed costs + variable costs = total costs.

5 Approach it step by step, plotting one line at a time. Plot the fixed costs line first as this acts as a double check for the position where total costs start.

Answers

1 a) flow or mass **b)** batch **c)** fixed, variable, variable **d)** i) £30 000 ii) £10 000 iii) £30 000
break-even chart for **1d)**:

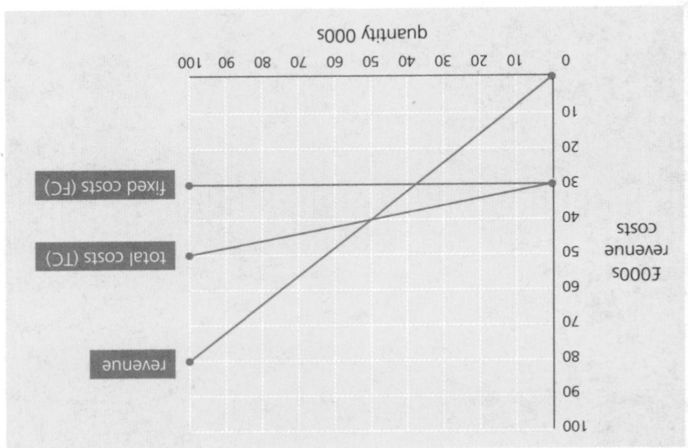

Finance

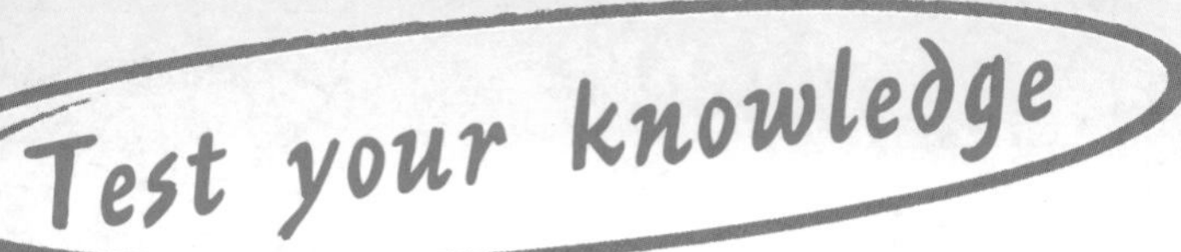

1 What is the purpose of a cash flow forecast?

2 State two benefits of producing budgets.

3 "Lagarde" is a French bistro owned by a sole trader. It requires finance in order to purchase a new range. This will cost £4500. The business does not have the funds to purchase the range. Advise Frédérique, the owner, of the sources of finance which could be considered.

4 State two factors which should be considered when deciding upon a source of finance.

Answers

1 to assist in planning / a cash flow forecast can identify when an overdraft will be required / this can help to ensure the survival of a business **2** to help meet business objectives, motivate employees, provide a target to achieve **3** the owner could consider a bank loan or hire purchase **4** length of time needed, reason needed, type of business, amount required

Finance

Improve your knowledge

1 **Cash flow** is the amount of money (cash) moving into the business (inflows) minus the amount moving out of the business (outflows). Cash flow statements provide historical information which can be used to help plan for the future. The best way to plan ahead is to produce a **cash flow forecast.** This is a prediction of the likely inflows and outflows for a stated period of time in the future, e.g. one year. By producing a cash flow forecast it is possible to identify when an overdraft will be required.

Cash flow forecast	Jan. £	Feb. £	March £
Inflows			
Sales	8000	13 500	17 000
Total inflows	8000	13 500	17 000
Outflows			
Rent	2000	2000	2000
Salaries	3050	3050	3500
Raw materials	3000	4000	9000
Heating and lighting	200	200	200
Total outflows	8250	9250	14 700
Surplus (deficit)	(250)	4250	2300
Balance carried forward	(4200)	(4450)	(200)
Net cash flow	(4450)	(200)	2100

This forecast shows that an overdraft is required in January and February. You may have to draw a cash flow chart based on information given. Remember that cash flow is ongoing so the amount carried forward has to be included.

2 **Budgets** consider forecast sales and forecast costs. These are set for the business as a whole but also broken down so that individual departments know what they have to achieve. For example, one shop which is part of a chain will have a budget for the branch and within that budgets for salaries, sales etc.

Budget setting can help a business achieve its objectives. When actual sales are lower than budgeted sales remedial action can be taken. In the same way if too much money is being spent on overtime this can be reduced.

Budgets can be used to motivate employees, for example achieving or exceeding a sales budget may carry a financial reward.

3 **Sources of finance**

Creditor – the business that has given credit or is owed money.

Debtor – the business that has borrowed the money or received goods on credit.

All businesses require finance, either when they are being set up, to fund expansion, or to assist cash flow.

Loan – a fixed sum of money borrowed from a bank for a fixed period of time. Interest has to be paid on the loan. Used to buy assets.

Overdraft – a facility available from the bank. The business can withdraw money from their account (when there isn't any money in the account) up to an agreed level, e.g. £2000. Interest is only paid on the amount borrowed, but repayable on demand. An overdraft is often used to cover short-term cash flow problems.

Own savings – may be used when setting up a business. This method is suitable for sole traders. It is easy to arrange, but may not provide sufficient funds.

Family and friends – may be suitable for sole traders, small partnerships, private limited companies. The amount of money available may be limited.

Trade credit – offered by most businesses. Goods may be taken or delivered with payment due 30 days later. The number of days depends on the agreement. For example, a clothes shop could buy dresses on 30 days' credit, sell them and pay the supplier (creditor) using the money generated through selling the dresses to the general public.

Retained (internal) profit – money which the business has kept. It is inexpensive and in many cases the preferable source of finance if available.

Hire purchase – a hire purchase agreement allows the buyer to obtain the product immediately by hiring or borrowing it, whilst paying for it in instalments. Interest is charged but it does enable the business to have use of the item straight away.

Leasing – the business has use of the product but does not own it. A monthly sum is paid in order to have use of the product. Many businesses lease photocopiers. Leasing is suitable for products which may be required for a short period of time or which are technically improved on a regular basis.

Factoring – if trade credit is given to another business but the money is required before the end of the credit period the debt can be sold to a factoring firm. This firm will pay the creditor immediately, but not as much as the debt. The factoring firm then collect the debt in full when it is due.

Shares – only available to companies. Private limited companies cannot publicly offer shares for sale. Plcs can offer shares through the Stock Exchange. Control can be lost.

Debentures – sold on the Stock Exchange, but this is a loan with a fixed return for the debenture holder, unlike shareholders who receive a dividend.

Grants from EU or government – may be difficult to obtain as there are qualifying criteria but they are cheap.

Factors affecting choice

These include:

- type of business
- length of time required – loans long term, overdrafts short term
- amount required
- what it is needed for – is it risky?

Now learn how to use your knowledge

Use your knowledge

1 Eleanor and Matthew Greaves are directors at Kendal Clothing Ltd. They have just received an order from a new customer for 5000 skirts. They are able to use their existing machinery to fulfil this order but need to employ 30 temporary employees. If the customer is pleased they will place orders of similar quantities every two months but they require 60 days' credit. Eleanor and Matthew will have to pay the temporary employees weekly but until they are paid by their customer will not have the funds to do so. *Hint 1*

a) Advise Eleanor and Matthew of a suitable source of finance for paying the temporary employees. ____________________

b) Explain why this source of finance is suitable.

____

____

____

c) Kendal Clothing Ltd require a photocopier. They are considering leasing or hire purchase. State **one advantage** and **one disadvantage** for each. *Hint 2*

Leasing – advantage ________________________________

____

____

Leasing – disadvantage ______________________________

____

____

Hire purchase – advantage ______________________

____

____

Hire purchase – disadvantage ______________________

____

____

2 Below is a table stating features of different sources of finance. Complete the blank boxes using the list that follows the table.

Feature of source of finance	Source of finance
Not available to sole traders or partnerships	
Sold on the stock exchange with a fixed return	
Offered to other businesses who buy goods	
The debt is sold and a payment received immediately	

Trade credit
Factoring
Debenture
Shares

3 What is a cash flow forecast? *Hint 3*

____

____

4 When would a bank manager want to see a cash flow forecast? *Hint 4*

____

____

____

____

Hints and answers follow

Finance

1 This is a short-term need for finance.

2 One of the options enables the business to keep the photocopier.

3 A forecast is a prediction.

4 A bank manager needs information to help him or her decide whether lending money is wise. Will the debt be repaid?

Answers

1 a) overdraft **b)** the finance is required for short period of time in order to pay wages / once the customer has paid Kendal Clothing Ltd the overdraft can be cleared / interest will only be paid on the amount used **c) leasing** advantage: able to change it for a better model when designs change, disadvantage: will not own the photocopier / **hire purchase** advantage: photocopier will belong to the business when all payments have been made, disadvantage: interest is charged or improved models may be developed and become available before payments are complete **2** shares, debenture, trade credit, factoring **3** an estimate or prediction of the inflows and outflows of cash for a stated period of time / it also details the net cash flow which shows whether the business is likely to have a surplus or deficit at any give time **4** a bank manager would want to see a cash flow forecast when deciding whether to allow an overdraft / a cash flow forecast would indicate the business is planning ahead and should demonstrate where there is a need for an overdraft / the figures on the cash flow forecast would have to be substantiated in some way, for example, if it shows an increase in sales, evidence should support this

Profit and loss, balance sheets and analysis

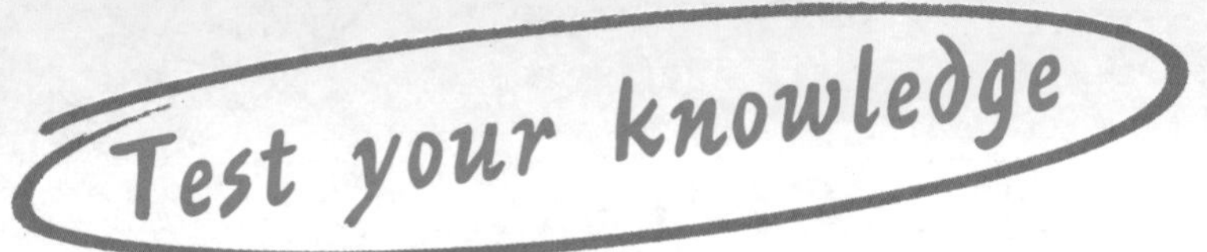

1. State the calculation used to determine cost of sales.

   ______________________________________.

2. How is gross profit calculated?

   ____

   How is net profit calculated?

   ____

3. Corporation tax is paid out of ________ __________________.

4. What does a balance sheet show?

   ____

5. Machinery is an example of a ___________ asset. Stock is an example of a ______________ asset.

6. The value of investment by shareholders as shown on a balance sheet is _____________ _____________.

7. The working capital ratio is ______________________________.

   The calculation for gross profit margin is ___________________________ .

Answers

1 opening stock + purchases – closing stock **2** subtracting cost of sales from sales revenue / subtracting expenses from gross profit **3** net profit **4** what a business owes and owns at a precise point in time **5** fixed, current **6** share capital **7** current assets : current liabilities, $\frac{\text{gross profit} \times 100}{\text{turnover}}$

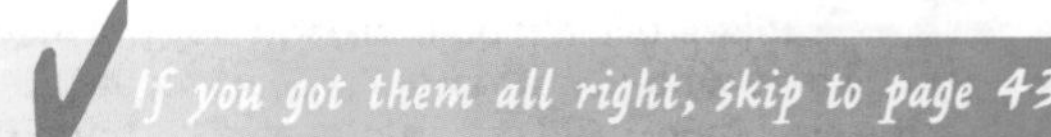

Profit and loss, balance sheets and analysis

Improve your knowledge

1 **Trading** and **profit and loss accounts** show gross and net profit. It represents a period of time such as one year.

Cost of sales = opening stock + purchases – closing stock.

2 **Gross profit** = sales revenue minus cost of sales.

Net profit = gross profit minus expenses.

Expenses = costs incurred in running the business, e.g. wages and salaries, rent, heating and lighting.

Shearcross Farm Enterprises Ltd

Trading profit and loss account for year ending 31 December 1998

Sales revenue		250 000
less cost of sales		75 000
Gross profit		175 000
Expenses		
Wages and salaries	50 000	
Rent	12 000	
Heating and lighting	1 000	
Vehicles	10 000	
Stationery	2 000	
Insurance	2 000	
	77 000	
Net profit		98 000

3 **Corporation tax** (tax on profit paid to the state) and **dividends** (paid to shareholders as a return on their investment) are paid out of net profit. The amount left is known as retained profit. This can be used to help fund expansion or investment.

Shearcross Farm Enterprises Ltd

Balance sheet as at 31 December 1998

	£	£	£
Fixed assets			
Buildings	150 000		
Machinery	45 000		
		195 000	
Current assets			
Stock	30 000		
Debtors	15 000		
Cash	15 000		
		60 000	
less			
Current liabilities			
Trade creditors	20 000		
Tax owed	10 000		
Dividends payable	15 000		
		45 000	
Net current assets		15 000	
Net assets			210 000
Financed by			
Share capital	100 000		
Reserves	50 000		
Loan capital	60 000		
Capital employed			210 000

4 A **balance sheet** shows what the business owes and owns at a precise point in time and is based on the fact that total assets must equal total liabilities (net assets employed = capital employed).

5 **Fixed assets** – items that are owned by the business and will be used for a long time. Fixed assets usually have a high value, e.g. machinery. Buying fixed assets is **capital expenditure**.

Current assets – items that are owned by the business but will probably be converted into cash before the date of the next balance sheet, e.g. stock, debtors, cash.

Current liabilities – money that is owed by the business to creditors but will probably be paid before the date of the next balance sheet, e.g. goods supplied on trade credit, rent owing, tax.

Total assets = fixed assets + current assets.

6 **Capital** – total value of the business.

Share capital – total value of investment by shareholders.

Capital employed – total value of long-term finance, e.g. loans.

Depreciation – over time, fixed assets lose their value. If the fixed asset was sold, it would not generate the original purchase price. To account for this, the business reduces its value on the balance sheet through depreciation.

7 **Analysis**

a) **Turnover** is the revenue from sales for the period of the trading profit and loss account.

b) **Profitability**

Gross profit margin

$$\frac{\text{gross profit}}{\text{turnover}} \times 100$$

shows gross profit as a percentage of sales. A business would want to maintain or increase this percentage.

Net profit margin

$$\frac{\text{net profit}}{\text{turnover}} \times 100$$

shows net profit as a percentage of sales. Again business would want to maintain or increase this percentage.

Return on capital employed

$$\frac{\text{net profit}}{\text{capital employed}} \times 100$$

shows the percentage rate of return for the owners' investment.

c) **Liquidity**

Working capital ratio shows whether a business can pay its short-term debts. Current assets : current liabilities. Current assets should be greater than current liabilities.

Acid test ratio (liquid capital) shows whether a business can pay its short-term debts *without* selling stock. This is important as a business may not be able to sell stock quickly.

Current assets less stock : current liabilities.

Now learn how to use your knowledge

Profit and loss, balance sheets and analysis

Use your knowledge

1 On the balance sheet below, complete the missing figures A, B, C and D. *Hint 1*

AbaChem Ltd
Balance sheet as at 31 December 1998

	£	£	£
Fixed assets			
Buildings	130 000		
Machinery	40 000		
		A______	
Current assets			
Stock	25 000		
Debtors	10 000		
Cash	12 000		
		B______	
less			
Current liabilities			
Trade creditors	15 000		
Tax owed	C______		
Dividends payable	17 000		
		42 000	
Net current assets		5 000	
Net assets			175 000
Financed by:			
Share capital	100 000		
Reserves	45 000		
Loan capital	30 000		
Capital employed			D______

2 When sales are £450 000, cost of sales are £200 000. Calculate the following (show your workings): *Hint 2*

a) Gross profit. ______________________________

b) Gross profit margin. ______________________________

c) Assuming that expenses are £125 000, calculate net profit.

____

d) What is the net profit margin? ______________________________ *Hint 3*

____

3 a) What is the working capital ratio? ______________________________ *Hint 4*

b) Why does a business use the working capital ratio?

____

____

4 Why are retained profits important to a business? *Hint 5*

____

____

____

Hints and answers follow

Profit and loss, balance sheets and analysis

1 Follow the balance sheet logically from the top down, adding up each section of figures. Total net assets = capital employed.

2 Gross profit = sales revenue – cost of sales.

3 Net profit = gross profit – expenses.

4 Working capital ratio is current assets : current liabilities.

5 Retained profits are kept within the business. What could they be used for?

Answers

1 A £170 000 **B** £47 000 **C** £10 000 **D** £175 000 **2 a)** £250 000 **b)** 55.5% **c)** £125 000 **d)** 27.8%
3 a) current assets : current liabilities **b)** to see if the business can pay its short-term debts
4 retained profits can be used as a source of finance to fund expansion, to invest in research and development or to invest in new machinery

People

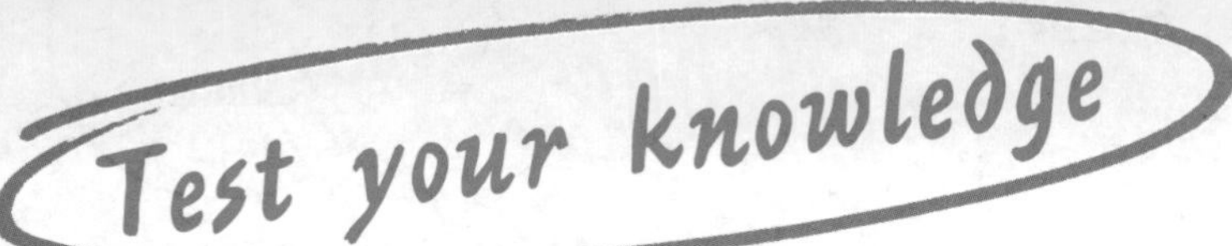

1 A ______________ contract of employment continues indefinitely.

2 ______________ rate is paid for the number of hours worked.

3 An additional payment for achieving a sale is ______________ .

4 State two deductions from pay. ______________ ______________ ,
______________ ______________ .

5 Staff discount and a company car are examples of ______________
______________ .

6 The purpose of a person specification is to ______________________
____

7 Two methods of applying for a job are by ______________
______________ and ______________ .

8 ______________ training is given to new recruits.

Answers

1 permanent **2** time **3** commission **4** income tax, national insurance, donation to charity, contribution to pension scheme or share option scheme, trade union subscription, company loan repayment **5** fringe benefits **6** state the qualifications and experience which are essential or desirable for the job holder **7** application form, c.v. **8** induction

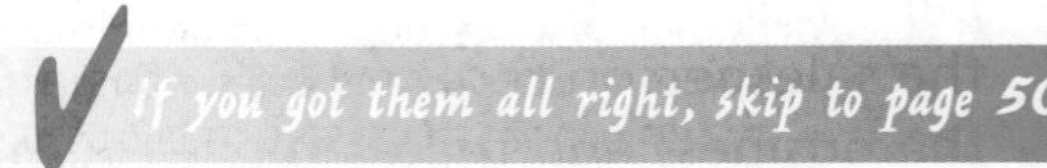

People

Improve your knowledge

1 Employees may work **full-time** (approx. 37.5 hours) or **part-time** (a proportion of the full-time hours). A contract of employment may be **permanent** (continues indefinitely), **fixed-term** (for a stated period of time, e.g. one year) or **temporary** (for a short-term need, e.g. to cover holiday absence). When two or more people share one job and split the hours this is known as a **job share**. **Flexi-time** allows employees to work their standard number of hours but with the option to vary the times these hours are worked, e.g. starting early and leaving early or working longer hours Monday to Thursday and taking Friday afternoon off. Flexi-time is not suitable for all jobs, e.g. nurse or teacher.

2 Most people work to earn money.

Salaries are paid monthly. **Wages** are paid weekly.

Time rate is paid for the number of hours worked and is normally paid at an hourly rate, e.g. £4.00 per hour.

Piece rate is paid for the number of products or components made, e.g. 60p per component. Costs are kept in line with production but quality sometimes decreases.

Flat rate is a fixed amount regardless of the amount of hours worked or time taken. Flat rate is normally paid to managers, e.g. £30 000 per annum.

3 **Overtime** is paid for time worked in addition to normal working hours, e.g. normally works 37.5 hours and works an extra 5 hours. Overtime is paid at a higher rate of pay. Double time is twice the normal rate of pay, time and a half is one and a half times the normal rate of pay.

Commission is additional money paid for achieving a sale. It is often paid as a percentage, e.g. product sold for £150, if commission is 10% the salesperson receives £15. It is an incentive to sell more and allows the business and the employee to benefit at the same time.

Bonus is an additional payment for achieving a specific goal, e.g. achieving a stock target, fulfilling a large order on time, improving quality.

Profit sharing is where employees receive a payment which varies according to the amount of profit the business has made. This encourages employees to work harder and reduce wastage to increase profits.

4 **Income tax** and **national insurance** are payable on earnings. They are normally deducted by the employer. Gross pay is the total pay before deductions, net pay is the amount actually received by the employee. Other deductions can include: trade union subscriptions, donations to charity, contributions to a pension scheme, contributions to a share option scheme.

5 **Fringe benefits** are additional benefits offered, which the company pays for or organises and from which the employee gains. Examples include discount on the firm's products; company car; life assurance; low interest loans and private health care.

Working conditions such as the temperature, amount of light, toilet facilities could also affect an employee's motivation. **Terms and conditions of employment** refers to job title, hours of work, rate of pay, benefits offered. This could also affect motivation.

6 If an employee leaves or a new position is created, a vacancy has to be filled. A **job description** is written which gives details of: job title; who the job holder reports to; who job holder is responsible for and a brief description of the duties involved. A **person specification** details the qualifications and experience which are essential or desirable for the post.

The vacancy is advertised using the information in the job description and person specification. It could be advertised **internally** (within the business) or **externally** (to the general public). External advertising could take place through job centres, newspaper advertisements, specialist magazine advertisements, Internet, sign at the factory gate or shop window.

Recruitment agencies offer a specialist recruitment service. This can be expensive but saves time as they place advertisements, deal with correspondence and conduct interviews. They are especially useful for recruiting temporary employees.

7 To apply for a vacancy applicants can fill in an **application form** or send a **curriculum vitae** (c.v.). The business produces the application form which consists of sections for the applicant to complete, such as name, address, date of birth, education, work experience. Application forms ensure that all applicants' details are received in a standard format which makes it easy to compare against the person specification. A c.v., which the applicant creates, will contain similar information and may be preferable for more senior positions when an application form may not hold sufficient detail.

Applications are **screened** and those who match the criteria in the person specification are short-listed and invited to attend an **interview**. The interview is a further screening process. Questions are asked to enable the interviewer to determine who is the most suitable applicant and the job is then offered to that person. The interview also enables the applicant to find out about the organisation and the job and helps them to decide if they would like to work there. A **reference** from a past employer gives information about time-keeping, what their job involved and how well they performed their duties.

8 **Induction training** is given to a new job holder. This could include: history of the business; tour of the premises; introduction to other employees; health and safety procedures including fire evacuation; being shown how to use machinery. Induction training helps new employees to settle and become effective quickly.

On-the-job training takes place at the normal place of work, e.g. being shown how to use machinery.

Off-the-job training takes place away from the normal place of work, e.g. attending a leadership skills course.

Internal training is conducted by another employee within the business, e.g. by a supervisor or training officer.

External training is conducted by someone who is not employed by the business, e.g. a college or training organisation.

Training helps to motivate employees, and improves skills and quality. It is an investment in the future of the business.

Now learn how to use your knowledge

People

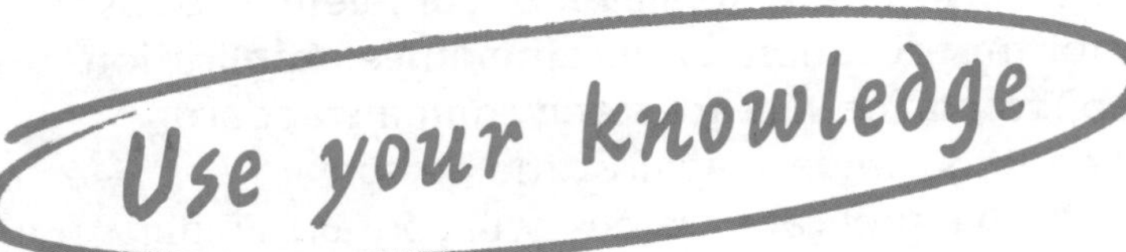

1 J. Sidhu Ltd manufacture garden tools such as forks, spades and rakes. The employees who make the tools are paid by time rate, while the sales force and managers are paid by flat rate.

a) What is meant by time rate? *Hint 1*

____

____

b) What is meant by flat rate? *Hint 1*

____

____

c) J. Sidhu Ltd have gained a new customer who insists on receiving orders more quickly than existing customers.

State which method of payment could increase the speed of the workers and one disadvantage of this method. *Hint 2*

Method ______________________________

Disadvantage ______________________________

d) The sales team gained the new customer. What incentive could be offered to generate more orders? Explain why this incentive is appropriate. *Hint 3*

Incentive ______________________________

Reason ______________________________

____

e) Sales have increased greatly. As a result there is a need to recruit three more employees to make the garden tools. Unemployment in the area is quite high and where possible the managing director prefers to recruit local people. State two methods of advertising the vacancies and explain why each is appropriate. *Hint 4*

Method 1 ______________________________

Explanation ______________________________

____

____

Method 2 ______________________________

Explanation ______________________________

____

____

f) Three new employees will be joining the company. The personnel manager is arranging their induction training. What is it likely to include?

____

____

State and explain how the new employees will benefit from induction training. *Hint 5*

____

____

g) What is meant by external training? *Hint 1*

____

____

Hints and answers follow

People

1 This is a straightforward definition.

2 Employees may be encouraged to work faster if they were paid for what they produce.

3 Most people are motivated by money. These people are selling, not producing.

4 Think of methods which would attract local people.

5 Starting a new job can be quite worrying as there is so much to learn.

Answers

1 a) employees are paid for the number of hours they work **b)** employees are paid the same salary regardless of the number of hours worked **c)** piece rate, the number of mistakes may increase causing the level of quality to decrease **d)** commission, encourages sales team to sell more products in order to earn more money / the business benefits as well through additional sales **e) method 1** job centre **explanation** – the vacancy will be seen there by local people, especially those who are unemployed / it is free to advertise at a job centre / **method 2** local newspaper **explanation** – it is fairly inexpensive to advertise in a local newspaper, and all three positions can be advertised together / local people who J. Sidhu Ltd are trying to recruit will read the newspaper / other examples include notice at factory gate, word of mouth **f)** a tour of the premises, introduction to other employees, health and safety requirements, how to operate machinery / it will help them to understand what their job involves and how the company operates, who to go to for help, how to find facilities such as toilets, canteen, what to do in the event of a fire / it should also help them to settle into their new job quickly **g)** training which is conducted by someone who is not employed by the business

Employee relations and communication

Test your knowledge

1 When a trade union negotiates and bargains on behalf of its members this is called ______ ______ .

2 State two benefits of belonging to a trade union.

______

______

3 State two examples of industrial action. ______ , ______

4 If an industrial dispute cannot be settled, who may be able to help? ______ .

5 If an employee believes that they have been unfairly dismissed, they can take their case to an ______ ______ .

6 Communication is effective if the message has been ______ and ______ by the recipient.

7 State four examples of written communication ______ ______ ______ ______ .

Answers

1 collective bargaining **2** collective bargaining, legal advice and support regarding employment issues, training and education, discounts in shops **3** strike, sit-in, go-slow, boycott, overtime ban, work-to-rule **4** ACAS **5** employment tribunal **6** received, understood **7** letter, memo, report, minutes, agenda, notice

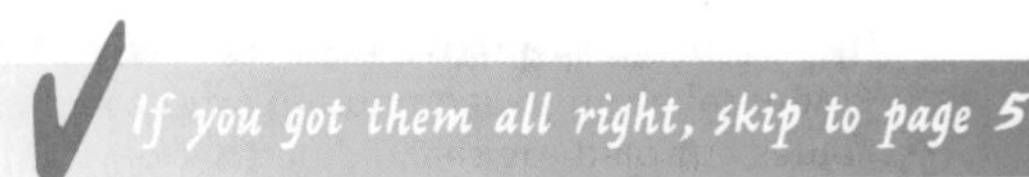

Employee relations and communication

Improve your knowledge

1 A **trade union** represents the interests of its members. **Collective bargaining** occurs when the trade union negotiates and bargains with the employer on behalf of the workers. **Individual bargaining** occurs when individuals negotiate and bargain with their employer. Collective bargaining agreements may cover rates of pay, hours of work, holiday entitlements, company sick pay schemes or redundancies.

2 In return for a **subscription**, members of trade unions receive many benefits in addition to collective bargaining: **legal advice and support** when facing disciplinary action, dismissal, unfair dismissal, sex or race discrimination, harassment; reduced rates for insurance; **discounts** in shops; **training and education**.

Benefits to employers of trade unions include: negotiations with one body rather than many individuals; trade unions can help implement change; unions have a knowledge of the business or industry which individuals may not have; trade unions may have more realistic expectations than individuals.

3 When negotiations have been unsuccessful, employees may take **industrial action** in order to persuade employers.

Strike – workers refuse to work. This may be for a short period of time, e.g. one day. A secret ballot has to be held before a strike can be called and the majority must be in favour for the strike to go ahead.

Sit-in – workers remain on the premises and refuse to leave. This action may be taken if a plant or business is due to close and jobs will become redundant.

Boycott – workers refuse to carry out a duty, perhaps because it is a new part of their job which they do not agree with.

Overtime ban – workers refuse to work any overtime, which can affect productivity and lead to loss of orders.

Work-to-rule – work according to every minor rule and regulation, which will slow down productivity. **Go-slow** has a similar effect when everything is done slowly.

4 If a dispute is not settled, assistance may be available. An **arbitrator** considers all the facts and decides on a fair outcome. A **conciliator** brings both sides together to help them resolve the problem themselves. **ACAS** (Advisory Conciliation and Arbitration Service) can help settle industrial disputes. ACAS also offer advice to individuals and businesses regarding employment rights.

Single union agreements are a feature of modern industrial relations. An employer agrees to recognise one trade union. It is easier to negotiate with one union than several who may have different expectations and priorities.

5 **Sex Discrimination Act** 1975 – discrimination on the grounds of gender or marital status is unlawful.

Race Relations Act 1976 – discrimination on the grounds of colour, race, nationality or ethnic or national origin is unlawful.

If discriminated against, individuals can take their case to an **employment tribunal**. If their case is proved there is no upper limit to the amount of compensation they can receive.

Employment tribunals also hear cases of unfair dismissal. An employment tribunal may decide that compensation should be paid, the person be reinstated (return to their old job) or re-engaged (employed by the same firm in a different position).

Health and Safety at Work Act 1974 – employers have to provide a safe work place for employees and visitors to the premises, e.g. providing safety equipment and clothing, maintaining machinery, ensuring fire exits are clear and evacuation procedures adequate. Employees also have an obligation to protect themselves and others by reporting dangers and accidents, wearing protective clothing etc. Having a safe environment reduces the risk of accidents and days lost through sickness. It helps motivate employees and gains the business a reputation as a good employer. The Factories Act 1961 and The Offices, Shops and Railway Premises Act 1963 also ensure that working conditions are safe and meet a minimum standard.

6 Communication

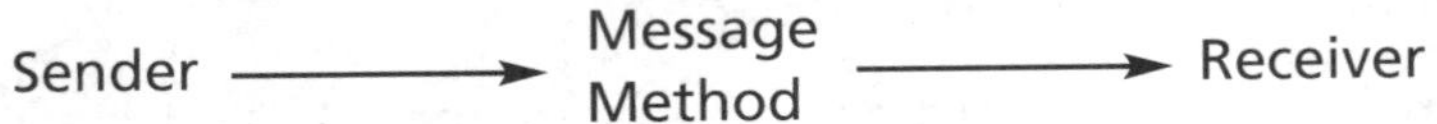

The type of communication varies according to who the sender is, what message has to be conveyed, how many people it is being sent to and who the receiver is. Effective communication improves motivation, ensures that business objectives are understood, and informs employees about their roles and responsibilities. Communication is only effective if a message has been **received** and **understood** by relevant personnel whether they are employees, customers or suppliers.

7 Types of Communication

Verbal – by telephone and face-to-face discussion (useful for one-to-one conversations), and meetings (good for informing a group but if there are too many people the message may not be heard properly or people may be afraid to ask questions).

Written – by letter, report, memos, notices, agenda (details of a forthcoming meeting), minutes (record of discussions at a meeting). Written communication is useful for imparting lengthy or detailed information. It also provides a record, e.g. a letter notifying an employee of a salary increase. A notice can display important information, e.g. evacuation procedure. Disadvantages include: the sender does not know if the message has been received or has been understood.

Electronic – by using a modem to send email (written messages are transferred immediately to the receiver, short or lengthy documents can be attached but a disadvantage is that many organisations and individuals still do not have email. Emails also have to be checked regularly for messages received). Shared servers allow information to be held on computer which can be accessed by others. This can be password protected for security reasons.

Visual – by graphs, charts, pictorial images, visual images. Signs often utilise visual communication as it is easily understood, e.g. no smoking sign. Video conferencing utilises verbal and visual communication.

Communication can be **internal**, within the organisation or **external**, between the organisation and the outside world.

Now learn how to use your knowledge

Employee relations and communication

Use your knowledge

1 The majority of employees at Harris Stationery plc belong to a trade union. The managers and union officials are holding discussions.

a) State **two** advantages to Harris Stationery plc of a trade union representing their employees. *Hint 1*

Advantage 1 ______________________________

____

Advantage 2 ______________________________

____

b) A machine operator has been dismissed. Fellow employees believe he has been unfairly dismissed and want him to be reinstated. They decide to take industrial action to try to achieve this. State two types of industrial action they could take and explain why each is suitable. *Hint 2*

Type of industrial action ______________________________

____

Explanation ______________________________

____

____

Type of industrial action ______________________________

____

Explanation ______________________________

____

____

c) Harris Stationery plc have appointed a female secretary. Michael Sunderland, an applicant whose experience was greater, was rejected as the interviewer felt the job was not suitable for a man. Explain why the company should not have rejected Michael and what may happen next.

Hint 3

____

____

____

____

____

____

d) Communication is effective if the message has been received and understood by the recipient. Notice-boards are often used to communicate to employees. State two disadvantages of this method of communication.

Hint 4

Disadvantage 1 ______________________________

____

Disadvantage 2 ______________________________

____

e) Email is becoming a popular way of communicating. State two advantages of communicating through email.

Hint 5

Advantage 1 ________________________________

____

Advantage 2 ________________________________

____

Hints and answers follow

Employee relations and communication

1. Discussions with one body are less time consuming than discussions with many individuals.

2. Most types of industrial action are suitable. What does the action involve and how will that affect the business?

3. What legislation protects Michael in this case?

4. How often do you look at notice-boards?

5. Email transfers written and visual information electronically via a modem and telephone line.

Answers

1 a) collective bargaining, trade unions can help to implement change **b) strike** – employees would stop working until Michael was reinstated / this would mean that products would not be manufactured so orders would not be fulfilled on time / the customers may find another supplier and Harris Stationery's revenue would fall, which could lead to a fall in profit / **go-slow** – the employees would still attend work and do their normal job but at a much slower pace / this could lead to a loss or reduction of orders, which would lead to a decrease in sales and profit / other answers include overtime ban and work to rule – the results would be similar **c)** the company should not have rejected Michael on the grounds of gender / sex discrimination is unlawful under the Sex Discrimination Act 1974 / Michael could take Harris Stationery plc to an employment tribunal for sex discrimination / if he succeeds, Harris Stationery plc will have to pay compensation **d)** the notice may not be seen or read, the person reading the notice may not understand or may misinterpret the information **e)** the message is transferred immediately, the message can be sent to many recipients at the same time, files or documents can be attached that have been produced on a computer

Growth, location and population

Test your knowledge

1 An ______________ is the overall goal of a business. To achieve this it sets ________________________________ .

2 When two firms join together this is called a ______________ .

3 When two firms join together from the same industry but different levels of the chain of distribution this is known as ______________ .

4 Define the term "economies of scale".

____

5 State two factors that may influence choice of location for a business.

____

____

6 When people leave this country to live in another country this is known as ______________ . When people leave another country to live in this country this is known as ______________ .

Answers

1 aim, objectives **2** merger **3** vertical integration **4** as output increases, unit costs decrease / this means that products can be made more profitably / this profit could be retained or the business could reduce its selling price which may increase the number of sales **5** geographical, personal reasons, proximity to raw materials or customers, industrial inertia, tradition, transport links, government policy **6** emigration, immigration

✓ If you got them all right, skip to page 63

Growth, location and population

Improve your knowledge

1 The overall goal that a business has is known as an **aim**. The aim of most firms is to provide a profit for its owners. **Objectives** are set which state how the aim can be achieved in general terms. Objectives are specific, e.g. to have 40% market share by December 2000. A **strategy** is a plan which details how the objectives can be achieved.

2 Growth is a common business objective. Size can be measured in many ways: profit, sales, number of units sold, number of employees, number of shops etc. Growth can be achieved through increasing sales to existing customers, selling to new customers, moving to larger premises or by acquisition.

Mergers take place when two or more firms join together and become one firm.

Takeovers are different from mergers in that one of the firms takes complete control over the other. A **hostile takeover** is where the firm does not want to be taken over. Plcs are susceptible to hostile takeovers as their shares can be bought on the Stock Exchange.

3 **Vertical integration** – two firms join together from the same industry but from different levels of production, e.g. manufacturer and retailer.

Horizontal integration – two firms join together from the same industry at the same level of production, e.g. retailer and retailer. When the level of production is the same and the products are related this is known as **lateral integration**.

Conglomerate integration – two firms join together vertically or horizontally from different industries, e.g. manufacturer of lampshades and manufacturer of soap powder. This helps to spread risks: if sales fall in lampshades, soap powder sales may not be affected.

4 **Economies of scale** can be achieved as a business grows. As output increases, unit costs fall. As each unit is cheaper to produce, the selling price can be reduced or a greater profit made. Examples include bulk buying, ability to raise finance and invest in more efficient equipment. If output increases too much, additional costs will be incurred on items such as new machinery, new premises. The unit cost will then increase and **diseconomies of scale** will occur.

5 There are many factors affecting choice of location.

Geographical – climate is important for agriculture.

Personal reasons – close to owner's home, owner likes area.

Raw materials – close to raw materials.

Customers – close to customers.

Industrial inertia – a business or industry remains in a site when the reason they located there has disappeared.

Tradition – the industry has always been in that location, e.g. The Potteries.

Transport links – sea, air, road or rail access may be relevant. Availability of **labour** due to unemployment rates or suitable qualifications.

Government/EU policy – the government or the EU can encourage businesses to set up in areas of high unemployment by offering incentives such as grants, rent free periods. E.g. enterprise zones where the infrastructure (power, roads, water etc.) is in place.

6 Population is an important consideration when deciding upon location and marketing plans. **Demography** is the study of population and considers total number of people, number in different geographical locations, age, gender, households, e.g. one person in a house or a family of five.

Population changes as:

- people die (measured through the **death rate**)
- people are born (measured through the **birth rate**)
- people move from this country to live in another country (**emigration**)
- people move from another country into this country to live (**immigration**).

Now learn how to use your knowledge

Growth, location and population

Use your knowledge

1 Peddie plc, who make curtains and blinds, are planning to expand their business by opening one additional factory. The Board of Directors are considering two locations: Salford, near Manchester, or Portsmouth on the south coast.

Salford	Portsmouth
high unemployment	low unemployment
low cost of living	high cost of living
enterprise zone	industrial estate
good access to motorways, rail	access to port, roads and rail

a) Which location would you advise the Board of Directors to choose? Explain why you are recommending this location. *Hint 1*

___

___

___

___

b) What are economies of scale? *Hint 2*

___

___

c) How may opening an additional factory cause diseconomies of scale? *Hint 3*

___

___

d) Peddie plc decide against opening another factory and are investigating other methods of growth. How does a merger differ from a takeover? *Hint 4*

____

____

e) Peddie plc decide to take over O'Brien Textiles plc, a manufacturer of bedding (sheets, pillow cases, duvet covers etc.). *Hint 5*

What type of integration is this? ____________________

State one benefit of this type of integration.

____

____

f) O'Brien Textiles plc do not want to be taken over. How can Peddie plc achieve the takeover? *Hint 6*

____

____

Hints and answers follow

Growth, location and population

1 What are the advantages and disadvantages of each location?

2 Scale refers to size of operations.

3 How will costs be increased?

4 What is the literal meaning of these words?

5 Bedding is a complementary product.

6 Remember both companies are public limited companies.

Answers

1 a) I would recommend Salford / recruitment would not be difficult as Salford has a high level of unemployment / it is conveniently located for road and rail networks which would ensure speedy receipt and delivery of goods / the enterprise zone offers benefits such as a rate free period
b) economies of scale are a reduction in unit cost as output or production increases
c) diseconomies of scale may occur as increased costs are incurred in new machinery, rent, power / although output will increase, unit costs will as well **d)** a merger occurs when two businesses join together, while a takeover occurs when one of the businesses has managerial control over the other **e)** lateral / the target market will be the same so economies of scale can be achieved through advertising **f)** by buying shares on the Stock Exchange

Influences on business

Test your knowledge

1 The ______________ ______ ______________ Act states that goods must be of merchantable quality.

2 Income tax is an example of ______________ taxation.

3 The increase in the level of prices is known as ______________ .

4 When unemployment is high, demand is ______________ .

5 Why are low interest rates preferred by many firms?

____

____

6 What is meant by automation?

____

____

7 When a new housing estate is built on fields at the edge of a town, an example of a social cost is ______________________________ .

An example of a social benefit is ______________________________ .

Answers

1 Sale of Goods **2** direct **3** inflation **4** low **5** when interest rates are low, the cost of borrowing is also low / loans help to fund investment in new technology, expansion, research and development **6** the use of machinery to replace people **7** loss of fields, noise and dirt while construction takes place / additional housing or larger population who will spend money in local shops thus helping the local economy

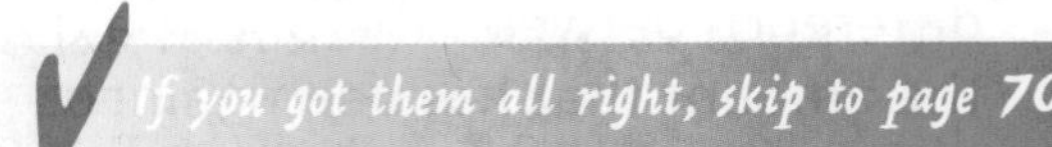

Influences on business

Improve your knowledge

1 Consumers are protected by legislation.

Sale of Goods Act 1979 states goods must be of merchantable quality (saleable and not faulty), be fit for the purpose for which they were sold – if sold as hiking boots they must be suitable for hiking, and correspond with the description given, e.g. on a label. The Supply of Goods and Services Act 1982 makes the same provisions for services.

Trade Descriptions Act 1968 legislates against a seller giving a false or misleading description of goods or services. This applies to written and verbal information.

Weights and Measures Act 1979 ensures that scales weigh correctly and measures, e.g. in pubs, are accurate.

Consumer Credit Act 1974 protects consumers who buy on credit or borrow money. Firms who offer credit must have a licence, state the annual percentage rate (APR).

2 The government obtains income through taxation.

Direct taxes – paid on income and wealth.

Income tax – paid by individuals on their income. If income tax is increased individuals will have less disposable income (money left to spend after all deductions from pay) and will spend less on goods and services. This will cause demand to fall and could result in a reduction in manufacturing which could in turn result in a rise in unemployment.

Corporation tax – paid by businesses on their profit. If firms have to pay more corporation tax they will have less to reinvest in the business.

Capital Gains Tax – paid on the sale of an asset. It is payable on the difference between the price paid and the price for which it was sold – the amount that has been gained.

Indirect taxes – paid on goods and services. The burden of indirect taxes can be passed on.

Value added tax (VAT) – paid on most goods and services. It is added at every stage of production and passed on to the consumer.

Customs duties – paid on goods imported.

Excise duties – paid on alcohol, tobacco and petrol.

3 **Inflation** is the increase in prices. As the price of raw materials increases, the selling price is increased to cover increased costs. Products in shops increase in price and consumers have to use more of their disposable income. The consumers then demand higher salaries and wages to maintain their standard of living. This further increases costs and so inflation continues.

4 **Unemployment** exists where people seeking work are unable to find employment. Unemployed people receive state benefits. This enables them to purchase essential goods and services but does not provide money for luxuries, so demand is **low**. By reducing the level of unemployment, more people will have a larger disposable income, therefore increasing demand. New Deal and Modern Apprenticeships are schemes which train unemployed people. The new skills and experience gained will enable them to apply for a wider range of jobs.

5 The level of **interest rates** will affect a business. Interest is charged as a percentage of a sum of money borrowed. If interest rates increase this means that it costs a business more to borrow, e.g. loans, overdrafts. Consumers are less likely to take out credit agreements or loans as it will cost more. If interest rates are high it also encourages saving.

6 **Technology** is changing and influencing business. Computer Aided Design (**CAD**) involves computers in designing many types of products. The products can be designed on screen and viewed from all angles before production commences. Computer Aided Manufacture (**CAM**) enables computers to be used in all aspects of manufacture including stock control and purchasing.

Automation is the use of machinery to replace people. Technology can speed up production and reduce costs through improved quality and fewer mistakes. Once the initial investment has been recovered it may be cheaper than employing people. Machines can work for longer periods of time and do not require breaks.

7 The community in which a firm operates can influence business activity. People living in a residential area close to a factory may complain about noise or air pollution. There may be social costs or benefits to business activity.

Private costs – costs to a business, e.g. investing in new machinery.

Private benefits – benefits to a business, e.g. increased turnover.

Social costs – costs to the community, individuals or society, e.g. pollution, loss of fields to industrial estates or shopping centres.

Social benefits – benefits to the community, individuals or society, e.g. employment, improved facilities.

Now learn how to use your knowledge

Influences on business

Use your knowledge

1 Jonathon Richards is employed by Columbus Ltd, a pet food manufacturer. He is paid a salary each month. *Hint 1*

Jonathon pays ______________ tax on his earnings.

Columbus Ltd pays ______________ tax on its profits.

2 Jonathon decides to spend some of his disposable income. He buys a video of a recently released film. When he plays the video it does not have sound. Why is Jonathon entitled to a refund? *Hint 2*

____

____

____

3 Columbus Ltd are considering investing in new technology. The firm will need a loan to fund the investment and interest rates have just risen. Why might this affect their decision to take a loan? *Hint 3*

____

____

____

4 Why does unemployment affect demand? *Hint 4*

____

____

____

5 After careful consideration Columbus Ltd decide to take a loan to finance investment in new technology which will be used on the production line and in the sales department. How will Columbus Ltd benefit from the use of new technology? *Hint 5*

____

____

____

6 Columbus Ltd are also looking for new premises. State which of the following are private costs or benefits and which are social costs or benefits. *Hint 6*

View from houses of a factory rather than fields. ______________

Increased market share. ______________

Buying a new factory. ______________

New jobs in an area of high unemployment. ______________

Hints and answers follow

Influences on business

1 The answers are corporation tax and income tax. Which way round do they go?

2 The video cassette is not working correctly. Was it saleable?

3 An increase in interest rates means that borrowing is more expensive.

4 Demand is a want backed up with the ability to pay.

5 Technology often increases the speed at which tasks are completed.

6 "Private" relates to the business.

Answers

1 income, corporation **2** under the Sale of Goods Act 1979 Jonathon is entitled to a refund as the video was not of merchantable quality **3** the rise in interest rates means that it will cost more to borrow the money needed for investment and Columbus Ltd will have to make sure that they can afford to repay the loan / a rise in interest rates may lead to a rise in the mortgage rate, which will mean that house owners will have less money to spend on luxuries and may not buy new pets **4** when people are unemployed they have a low level of income / this income must be spent on needs or essential goods and services rather than luxuries / if in paid employment the individual would probably have more disposable income which could be spent on more goods and services which would increase demand **5** new technology may increase the speed of production enabling orders to be supplied faster / this could lead to increased customer satisfaction / the quality of products may improve and the number of mistakes or faults decrease / the sales department will be able to keep computerised records of sales and customers, which will allow quick access to information and analysis **6** social cost, private benefit, private cost, social benefit

International trade

Test your knowledge

1. What is a multinational?

   ____

   ____

2. Products bought by this country from another country are ____________ .

   Products sold by this country to another country are ____________ .

3. If the exchange rate is lowered exports are ____________ and imports are ____________ .

4. What do the letters EU stand for? ____________ ____________ .

Answers

1 a firm which has bases, factories, plants, shops in more than one country **2** imports, exports **3** cheaper, dearer **4** European Union

International trade

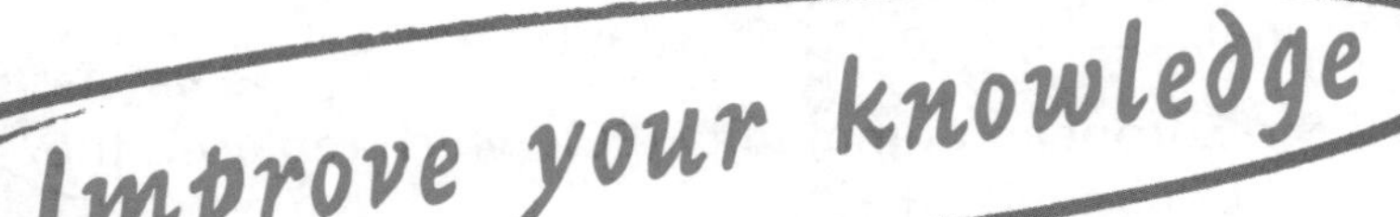

1 **Multinationals** are firms which have factories, bases, shops etc. in more than one country.

2 One country does not produce all the goods and services it requires. This may be because the climate is not suitable for certain crops, natural resources are not present or a greater selection of goods and services is desired.

Products brought into this country from another country are **imports**.

Products sold by this country to another country are **exports**.

When the product is a service, such as tourism, this is known as an **invisible import** or **invisible export**.

3 The **exchange rate** is the price at which one currency is exchanged for another. Products are paid for in the currency of the exporting country. Therefore a German car dealer buying a British car would pay in Pounds (£) not Deutschmarks (DM).

Example

£1 = 2DM A car sold at £10 000 costs 20 000DM

The exchange rate rises:

£1 = 3DM A car sold at £10 000 costs 30 000DM

The cost of exporting has increased. This may deter the German buyer from importing cars.

If the exchange rate is lowered exports are **cheaper** and imports are **dearer**.

If the exchange rate is raised exports are **dearer** and imports **cheaper**.

Following the Maastricht Treaty 1992, the **European Union (EU)** was formed. The member countries are: Austria, Belgium, Denmark, Finland, France, Germany, Greece, Italy, Ireland, Luxembourg, the Netherlands, Portugal, Spain, Sweden and the UK.

The EU replaced the European Community (EC), which replaced the European Economic Community (EEC).

The main aim of the EU is to bring about lasting peace and prosperity for all its citizens. To achieve this all barriers to trade between member countries have been removed. This means that goods, services, people and capital can be moved from one country to another.

Tariffs which are taxes on goods imported do not exist between member states.

Quotas are limits imposed on the quantity of a product imported. EU countries set quotas on products entering EU countries.

All products imported to an EU country from a non-EU country are subject to a **common external tariff**. Each member country charges the same amount of import tax.

European Monetary Union, where one currency will be used throughout member countries is under way. However, not all member countries have agreed to participate. The benefit of a single currency is that exchange rates will not be an issue in importing and exporting between member countries as there will be no need to exchange currencies.

The EU also influences business through employment legislation and grants to encourage firms to set up in areas of high unemployment.

Now learn how to use your knowledge

International trade

1 Crador plc manufacture cars. They have factories in three European countries. *Hint 1*

Are Crador plc:

a) a conglomerate

b) a multinational

c) state owned?

2 All three European countries belong to the EU. What does EU stand for? ______________ ______________ *Hint 2*

3 Crador plc do not have a factory in Germany and cars are exported there from the UK. The exchange rate is currently £1 = 2DM. The Finance Director anticipates an increase in the rate of exchange, and as a result he is calculating the price which the Germans will have to pay if the exchange rate changes to £1 = 2.5DM and £1 = 3DM. As an example he has selected a mid-range model at £12 000. *Hint 3*

a) Calculate the price of the car in DM when the exchange rate is

£1 = 2.5DM.

____

b) Calculate the price of the car in DM when the exchange rate is

£1 = 3DM.

____

c) Explain why the Finance Director would be concerned about a rising exchange rate.

Hint 4

d) The UK has opted out of the single European currency. Explain why the Finance Director is in favour of the UK joining the single currency.

Hints and answers follow

International trade

1 Multi means many.

2 You should be able to answer this automatically. If you can't, check point 4 in *Improve your knowledge*.

3 Price of the car in sterling x DM exchange rate.

4 What happens to the price of the car in Germany?

Answers

1 b) a multinational **2** European Union **3 a)** 2.5DM x £12 000 = 30 000DM **b)** 3DM x £12 000 = 36 000DM **c)** if the exchange rate increases this will also make exports more expensive than they are at the moment / a German car buyer may decide to purchase a car from another manufacturer as it will be cheaper / this will result in fewer cars being sold / as sales decrease this may lead to job losses as fewer employees will be required **d)** if the UK joined the single currency then problems associated with exchange rates would not exist when trading within the EU / sales would not fluctuate with changes in exchange rates and planning would be easier

Management

1. State two benefits of specialist departments.

____

____

2. Why may a new employee want to see an organisation chart?

____

____

3. What is a span of control?

____

4. The line of authority running from the top of an organisation to the bottom is called the ____________ ____ ____________ .

5. State one benefit to a subordinate of delegation.

____

6. A ____________ organisation is one where decision making is passed down the chain of command.

7. An ____________ leader makes all decisions without consultation.

Answers

1 experts' skills are available, employees can concentrate on one area of work **2** to see who's who in the organisation, to see how their role fits in **3** the number of employees who directly report to a superior **4** chain of command **5** the subordinate can develop new skills and experience **6** decentralised **7** autocratic

Management

Improve your knowledge

1 Larger firms have departments or functions which are responsible for different aspects of business activity. The main departments are as follows:

- **Finance Department** – responsible for budgets, cash flow, balance sheets, trading profit and loss accounts, payment to suppliers, receipts of payment by customers.
- **Marketing Department** – responsible for market research, promotion including advertising, brand image, pricing.
- **Personnel** or **Human Resources Department** – responsible for recruitment and selection, terms and conditions of employment, issuing contracts of employment, training, appraisals, dismissals including redundancy.
- **Production Department** – responsible for manufacturing goods and stock control. Service industries, such as retail, often have **operations departments** which are responsible for branch operations.
- **Sales Department** – responsible for selling products in the highest quantities possible to a variety of customers.

Benefits of specialist departments:

- **experts** in area
- experienced at this type of work
- hold relevant qualifications
- allows all employees to **concentrate on one area of work**.

2 An **organisation chart** shows which departments a business has and the job titles that exist in each department. It shows the relationship between employees. It shows who reports to whom and allows employees to see where their role fits in to the organisation as a whole.

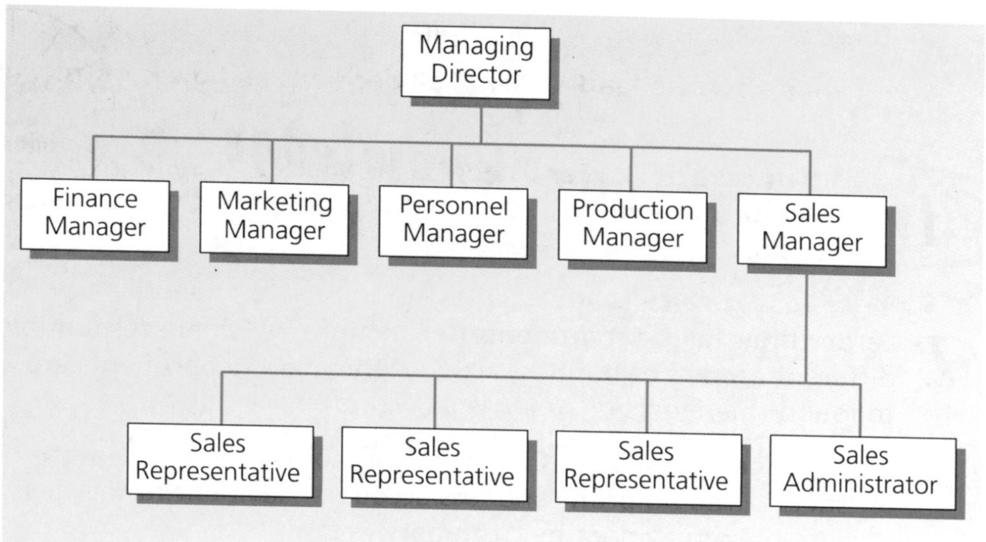

3 The **span of control** is the *number* of employees who report directly to another employee, e.g. in the organisation chart above, the span of control of the Managing Director is five, the span of control of the Sales Manager is four.

4 The **chain of command** is the line of authority which runs from the top of an organisation to the bottom, e.g. the Sales Representative and Sales Administrator report to the Sales Manager who reports to the Managing Director. The chain of command can be used to communicate information. Communication problems may occur if the chain of command is very long.

5 **Delegation** occurs when a task or duty is given to a subordinate to carry out. The subordinate is also given the necessary authority to perform that task or duty. Effective delegation can motivate employees and develop their skills, whilst at the same time allowing the person who is delegating more time to concentrate on other aspects of his or her job.

6 A **centralised organisation** is one where decisions are taken by senior employees often at a head office, e.g. stock is ordered for a chain of shops by a buyer at head office. A **decentralised organisation** is one where decision making is passed down the chain of command to employees who hold more junior positions.

7 There are three types of leadership style:

- an **autocratic leader** makes all decisions and gives instructions to subordinates
- a **democratic leader** listens to the views and opinions of subordinates and takes these into consideration when making decisions
- a ***laissez-faire* leader** allows employees to make their own decisions without interference.

In reality, managers or supervisors will often demonstrate a combination of these styles depending upon the situation.

Now learn how to use your knowledge

Management

Use your knowledge

1 Biento Ltd is a chain of retail outlets which specialise in selling posters, cards and stationery. The organisation chart is as shown below.

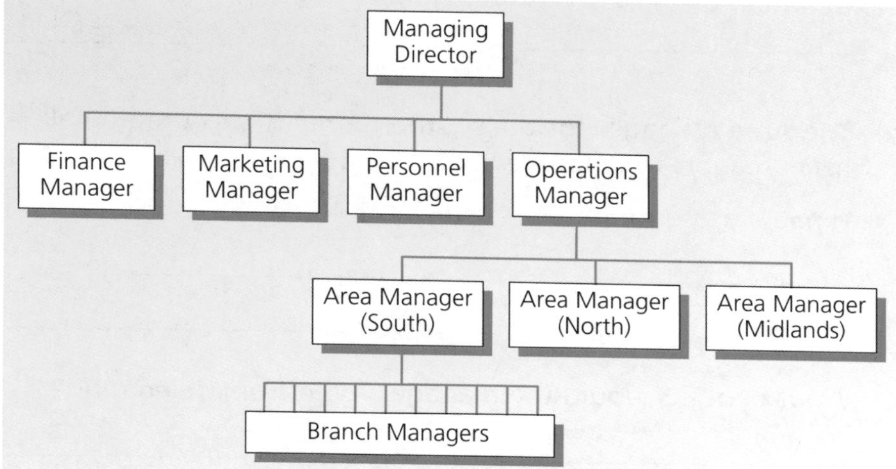

a) Why may Biento Ltd benefit from having a specialist Personnel Department?

____

____

b) The branch managers are responsible for buying stock, recruiting their staff, nominating staff to attend training courses and deciding where to display goods. Would you describe this as a centralised or decentralised organisation?

____

c) Referring to the organisation chart, what is the span of control of the Operations Manager? ______________

d) The branch managers all have differing leadership styles. *Hint 3*

The Manager of the branch in Liverpool encourages her sales assistants to offer ideas on how to improve sales and asks their opinion when changing the layout of the shop. What type of leadership style does this manager have?

____

The Manager of the branch in Hounslow makes decisions herself and informs the sales assistants of the decisions. She makes a list of jobs for each person to do during the day. What type of leadership style does this manager have?

____

e) The Area Manager for the southern area is encouraging all his managers to delegate. *Hint 4*

What is delegation?

____

____

What benefits would the managers gain from delegating?

____

____

____

____

Hints and answers follow

Management

1. Employees in the Personnel Department will be experts.
2. The span of control is always a number.
3. Leadership styles are democratic, autocratic and *laissez-faire*.
4. How would a manager benefit from having less to do?

Answers

1 a) a specialist personnel department would have employees who are trained and qualified in recruitment and selection, training, and would be aware of employment legislation including Health and Safety requirements / they would be able to offer advice to managers and staff regarding their terms and conditions of employment / this would mean that other employees could concentrate on their own job / the company would be less likely to have cases made against them in an employment tribunal which would incur costs **b)** decentralised **c)** three **d)** democratic, autocratic **e)** delegation is giving a subordinate a task or duty to perform / the necessary authority is also given to the subordinate / managers would benefit from delegation in several ways – by delegating routine tasks such as paperwork, they would have more time to concentrate on other aspects of their job, such as looking at how to increase sales or reduce costs / the managers may also benefit from having employees who are more highly motivated and able to take responsibility in their absence

Mock exam

1 Tyldesley Ltd manufacture mirrors. For some time David, the founder and main shareholder of the business, has been concerned about rising costs. Garner plc, a manufacturer of picture frames, wishes to take over Tyldesley Ltd and has offered to buy David's shares in the business.

a) What is meant by "shareholder"?

____ **(2)**

b) Garner plc believe that they can achieve economies of scale if they takeover Tyldesley Ltd. What is meant by economies of scale?

____ **(2)**

c) Explain how a takeover differs from a merger.

____ **(2)**

d) The managing director of Garner plc is an autocratic leader.

i) What is meant by the term autocratic leader? **(2)**

ii) State and explain one disadvantage of an autocratic leadership style.

Disadvantage ________________________________

Explanation ________________________________ **(3)**

iii) State and explain one advantage of a democratic leadership style.

Advantage ________________________________

Explanation ________________________________ **(3)**

[14]

2 David decides to review some figures before making a final decision.

	1997	**1998**
Sales	£500 000	£510 000
Cost of sales	A	£150 000
Gross profit	£400 000	B
Expenses	£200 000	£220 000
Net profit	C	£140 000

a) Fill in the missing figures A, B and C in the table above. **(3)**

b) Calculate the net profit margin in 1998.

____ **(2)**

c) Sales in 1998 have increased compared to 1997. Using the figures in the table explain why David is not happy about the financial position of the business.

____

____ **(4)**

d) State **two** examples of a fixed cost and **two** examples of a variable cost that Tyldesley Ltd may have.

Fixed cost ____

Fixed cost ____

Variable cost ____

Variable cost ____ **(4)**

e)

Output	Fixed costs £	Variable costs £	Total costs £	Revenue £
0	20 000	nil	20 000	nil
200	20 000	10 000	30 000	20 000
400	20 000	20 000	40 000	40 000
600	20 000	30 000	50 000	60 000

The table above shows costs and revenues for varying levels of output. Using this information, plot a break-even chart.

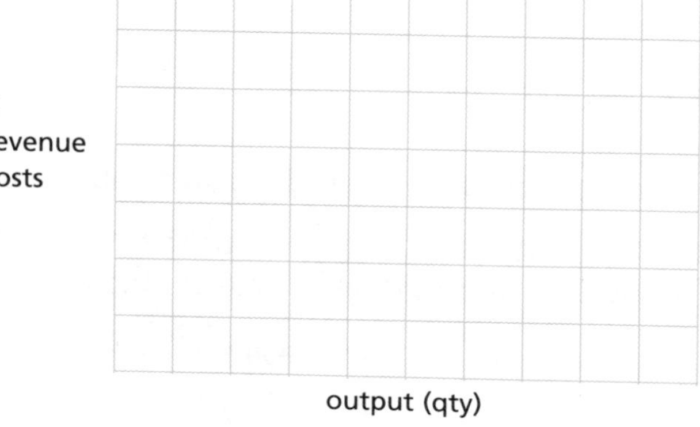

(6)

f) What is the break-even output? **(1)**

[20]

3 David Tyldesley has decided to sell his shares to Garner plc and resign from Tyldesley Ltd. With the money received from the sale of the shares David intends to open a bookshop as a sole trader.

a) David has found a suitable shop unit. Before deciding on the range of books to offer David carries out some market research.

i) What is market research?

____

____ **(3)**

ii) Why would it be important for David to continue to carry out market research after the shop opens?

____

____ **(3)**

iii) State two sources of information that would be available to David after the shop opens and explain why this information would be valuable.

____

____ **(6)**

b) Suggest a suitable method of advertising the new shop opening and explain why this method would be appropriate.

Method ______________________________________ **(1)**

Explanation __________________________________ **(3)**

c) David intends to offer a sales promotion for the first week that the shop is open. Suggest a suitable sales promotion and explain why this would be appropriate.

Sales promotion ______________________________ **(1)**

Explanation __________________________________ **(3)**

[20]

4 David will use his own savings to invest in the bookshop.

a) He will need additional sources of finance for the items listed below. For each item suggest an appropriate source of finance.

Shelving ____________________________________

Books (stock) ________________________________

Cash register ________________________________

Salaries for the first month's trading ____________ **(4)**

b) Why would David require additional finance in order to pay salaries for the first month? ______

______ **(2)**

c) The books can be bought directly from the publisher or from a wholesaler. What is a wholesaler? ______

______ **(2)**

d) Tyldesley Ltd was a private limited company. David Tyldesley is now a sole trader.

i) As a shareholder of Tyldesley Ltd David had limited liability. What is meant by limited liability? ______

______ **(3)**

ii) State and explain two advantages of sole traders.

Advantage ______

Explanation ______ **(4)**

Advantage ______

Explanation ______ **(4)**

[19]

5 David will be the manager of the bookshop.

a) David draws up a job description and person specification for a sales assistant.

i) What is a job description? ______

______ **(2)**

ii) What is a person specification? ______

______ **(2)**

b) Suggest **two** places where David could advertise for sales assistants. Explain why you have suggested each place.

Place 1 ______

Explanation ______

______ **(3)**

Place 2 ______

Explanation ______

______ **(3)**

c) State two methods of application ______________________________

____ **(2)**

d) David receives a large number of applications. He draws up a short list of applicants to interview. What are the benefits of an interview to:

i) David? ____

____ **(3)**

ii) the applicants? ______________________________________

____ **(3)**

e) The sales assistants will be paid time rate. What is time rate?

____

____ **(2)**

f) All new sales assistants will receive induction training. How will the business benefit from this?

____

____ **(4)**

[24]

6 a) A customer buys a book which is later found to have several pages missing. Explain how the customer is protected under consumer protection legislation.

____

____ **(3)**

b) One year after the shop opens, interest rates increase. Explain why David is concerned about the effect this will have on sales.

____

____ **(4)**

c) David decides to invest in EPOS – electronic point of sale. This is a cash register combined with a stock control system. As a sale is made, the stock level for that book is adjusted. What are the benefits to business of this new technology?

____

____ **(4)**

[11]

Total marks 108

Answers

1 a) A shareholder is a person who owns shares in a private limited or public limited company. In return for the investment the shareholder receives a dividend.

b) Economies of scale are reductions in unit costs when output is increased.

c) In a takeover or a merger two or more firms join together and become one firm. However, in a takeover one of the firms takes complete managerial control over the other.

d) i) An autocratic leader makes decisions without consulting employees and issues instructions.

ii) **Disadvantage** the business will not benefit from the experience of subordinate employees.
Explanation the subordinates may have ideas on how to improve quality, reduce costs, improve working practices. The business could benefit from increased profits.

iii) **Advantage** improved motivation.
Explanation if the employees feel that their views and opinions are valued they are more likely to be motivated. This could increase productivity and profitability.

2 a) A £100 000 B £360 000 C £200 000

b) Net profit divided by sales revenue x 100 = 27%

c) Although sales have increased by £10 000, cost of sales have increased by £50 000 and expenses have increased by £20 000. Gross and net profit have both decreased by a larger amount than the increase in sales. The profitability of the business has decreased.

d) Fixed costs: rent, uniform business rate, salaries.
Variable costs: raw materials, piece-rate pay, overtime, heating and lighting.

e)

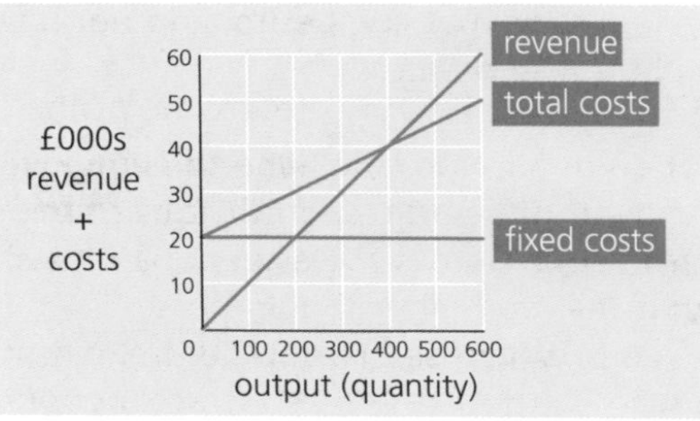

f) 400.

3 a) i) Market research is the gathering of information on customer views and preferences.

ii) To ensure that sales are maximised by offering the right product, at the right price, at the right time. Tastes and trends may alter and it is important to anticipate these changes.

iii) Sources of information include a breakdown of sales and feedback from customers. The sales information can highlight subject areas that are selling well or badly. Changes to the product mix could be made to improve sales. Once the shop is open, customers provide much information. This could be gathered informally, e.g. by noting down books that are requested but not stocked, or formally by questionnaire. The feedback from customers could also highlight training needs.

b) Advertisement in the local newspaper. The paper would be read by local people, who are also the target market. Details regarding shop name, address, telephone number, opening date, product range could be included. It could be referred back to if necessary. It is a cost effective method of advertising.

c) Discount voucher. A discount voucher could be included in the newspaper advertisement, whereby a 10% discount is offered on production of the voucher. This would encourage potential customers to visit the shop and buy a book. If impressed with the shop they would return to make future purchases.

4 a) Loan. Trade credit/overdraft. Loan/H.P. Overdraft.

b) The business may have cash flow problems in the first month due to the number of items which have to be bought at the same time, e.g. stationery, bags. Once trading, these would not have to be replaced at the same time.

c) A wholesaler acts as an intermediary between a manufacturer and a retailer. A wholesaler buys from several manufacturers and breaks bulk, enabling retailers to buy in smaller quantities from a variety of sources.

d) i) If the company goes into liquidation, shareholders' losses are limited to the value of their investment in the company. They will not lose personal possessions such as their home.

ii) Owner has control. The owner is able to make all decisions and does not have to consult others. This enables decisions to be made quickly.
Privacy. The sole trader does not have to publish accounts. This saves time and money and means that competitors do not have access to financial information about the business.

5 a) i) A job description details job title, who the employee is responsible to and for, and the main duties and responsibilities of the job holder.

ii) A person specification details the essential and desirable qualifications and experience that the job holder should possess.

b) Job Centre. It is free to advertise in a Job Centre, which makes it a cost effective way to recruit. The Job Centre attracts people looking for employment in the local area.

Local newspaper. The local paper is bought by people living in the area of the vacancy. It is relatively inexpensive and the advertisement can be cut out and retained.

c) Application form or curriculum vitae (c.v.).

d) i) It enables the interviewer to check details given on the application form or c.v., and to probe those areas in more depth. It enables other qualities to be assessed, for example David may be looking for sales assistants who are friendly and approachable. It is not possible to assess this on an application form.

ii) The applicant can find out more about the position, the firm, working conditions and terms and conditions of employment. The applicant may decide that it is not the type of firm that they would like to work for.

e) Time rate is a method of payment where employees are paid for the time that they work. Time rate is normally paid at an hourly rate of pay.

f) The employees will become effective in their role more quickly. This may mean that fewer mistakes are made, increased sales are made, and employees should have a greater understanding of their role. This would lead to increased profits. The employee is less likely to have an accident. The employee may be happy and decide not to leave.

6 a) The customer is protected under the Sale of Goods Act. The book has missing pages and is therefore not of merchantable quality. The customer is entitled to a refund.

b) When interest rates increase, the shop's customers may have less money to spend. If they have loans, the cost of borrowing will increase. It is likely that many of the customers will have mortgages. If the mortgage rate increases they will have less money to spend on wants and have to divert money to needs. The cost of credit will also increase, which may reduce the number of sales by credit card.

c) The introduction of EPOS will mean that fewer mistakes are made when using the till and in stock checking. Labour-saving computerised reports and analyses can be run. This means that more time can given to serving customers and increasing sales and therefore profit.